BOOK OF MORMON 2020

Come, Follow Me—
For Individuals and Families

Living, Learning, and Teaching the Gospel of Jesus Christ

D1607312

Published by
The Church of Jesus Christ of Latter-day Saints
Salt Lake City, Utah

© 2019 by Intellectual Reserve, Inc.
All rights reserved.
Version: 10/17
15155 000
Printed in the United States of America

Comments and corrections are appreciated. Please send them, including errors, to comefollowme@ChurchofJesusChrist.org.

Contents

Conversion Is Our Goal

The aim of all gospel learning and teaching is to deepen our conversion and help us become more like Jesus Christ. For this reason, when we study the gospel, we're not just looking for new information; we want to become a "new creature" (2 Corinthians 5:17). This means relying on Heavenly Father and Jesus Christ to help us change our hearts, our views, our actions, and our very natures.

But the kind of gospel learning that strengthens our faith and leads to the miracle of conversion doesn't happen all at once. It extends beyond a classroom into an individual's heart and home. It requires consistent, daily efforts to understand and live the gospel. True conversion requires the influence of the Holy Ghost.

The Holy Ghost guides us to the truth and bears witness of that truth (see John 16:13). He enlightens our minds, quickens our understandings, and touches our hearts with revelation from God, the source of all truth. The Holy Ghost purifies our hearts. He inspires in us a desire to live by truth, and He whispers to us ways to do this. Truly, "the Holy Ghost . . . shall teach [us] all things" (John 14:26).

For these reasons, in our efforts to live, learn, and teach the gospel, we should first and foremost seek the companionship of the Spirit. This goal should govern our choices and guide our thoughts and actions. We should seek after whatever invites the influence of the Spirit and reject whatever drives that influence away—for we know that if we can be worthy of the presence of the Holy Ghost, we can also be worthy to live in the presence of Heavenly Father and His Son, Jesus Christ.

Using *Come, Follow Me—For Individuals and Families*

Who Is This Resource For?

This resource is for every individual and family in the Church. It is designed to help you learn the gospel—whether on your own or with your family. If you haven't studied the gospel regularly in the past, this resource can help you get started. If you already have a good habit of gospel study, this resource can help you have more meaningful experiences.

How Should I Use This Resource?

Use this resource in any way that is helpful to you. You may find it helpful as a guide or aid for personal and family scripture study. You could also use it for family home evening. The outlines highlight important principles found in the Book of Mormon, suggest study ideas and activities for individuals and families, and provide places to record your impressions.

You and your family may already be studying the gospel regularly. For example, maybe you are reading scriptures other than the Book of Mormon for a seminary or institute class. *Come, Follow Me—For Individuals and Families* is not meant to replace or compete with the good things you are doing. There may be ways to learn from the Book of Mormon regularly and still accomplish your other scripture study goals. For example, you might read one book of scripture for your personal scripture study and read the Book of Mormon with your family (or vice versa). Follow the Spirit's guidance to determine how to approach your own study of the word of God.

How Does This Resource Relate to What Happens at Church?

The outlines in this resource are organized according to a weekly reading schedule. *Come, Follow Me—For Primary* and *Come, Follow Me—For Sunday School* follow the same schedule. To support your efforts to learn and live the gospel at home, your teachers at church will give you opportunities to share your experiences, thoughts, and questions about the scripture passages that you have been studying at home.

Because Sunday School is taught only twice a month, Sunday School teachers may choose to skip or combine outlines to keep up with the weekly schedule. This may also be necessary on weeks when regular Church meetings are not held because of stake conference or other reasons. During these weeks you are invited to continue to study the Book of Mormon at home.

Do I Need to Follow the Schedule?

The schedule will help you finish reading the Book of Mormon by the end of the year. In addition, following the same schedule as others in your ward can lead to meaningful experiences at church. But don't feel bound by the schedule; it is simply a guide to help you pace yourself. The important thing is that you are learning the gospel individually and as a family.

Ideas to Improve Your Personal Scripture Study

Here are some simple ways to enhance your study of the word of God in the scriptures.

Look for Truths about Jesus Christ

The scriptures teach us that all things testify of Christ (see 2 Nephi 11:4; Moses 6:63), so look for Him in the events, stories, and teachings of the Book of Mormon. Consider noting or marking verses that teach about the Savior and how to follow Him.

Look for Inspiring Words and Phrases

You may find that certain words and phrases in the scriptures impress you, as if they were written specifically for you. They may feel personally relevant and inspire and motivate you. Consider marking them in your scriptures or writing them in a study journal.

Look for Gospel Truths

Sometimes gospel truths (often called doctrine or principles) are stated directly, and sometimes they are implied through an example or story. Ask yourself, "What eternal truths are taught in these verses?"

Listen to the Spirit

Pay attention to your thoughts and feelings, even if they are unrelated to what you are reading. Those impressions may be the very things that your Heavenly Father wants you to learn.

Liken the Scriptures to Your Life

Consider how the stories and teachings you are reading apply to your life. For example, you could ask yourself, "What experiences have I had that are similar to what I am reading?" or "How can I follow the example of this person in the scriptures?"

Ask Questions as You Study

As you study the scriptures, questions may come to mind. These questions might relate to what you are reading or to your life in general. Ponder these questions and look for answers as you continue studying the scriptures.

Use Scripture Study Helps

To gain additional insights into the verses you read, use the footnotes, the Topical Guide, the Bible Dictionary, the Guide to the Scriptures (scriptures.ChurchofJesusChrist.org), and other study helps.

Consider the Context of the Scriptures

You can find meaningful insights about a scripture if you consider its context—the circumstances or setting of the scripture. For example, knowing the background and beliefs of the people a prophet spoke to can help you understand the intent of his words.

Record Your Thoughts and Feelings

There are many ways to record the impressions that come as you study. For example, you could mark a meaningful word or phrase and record your thoughts as a note in your scriptures. You could also keep a journal of the insights, feelings, and impressions you receive.

Study the Words of Latter-day Prophets and Apostles

Read what latter-day prophets and apostles have taught about the principles you find in the scriptures (for example, see conference.ChurchofJesusChrist.org and Church magazines).

Share Insights

Discussing insights from your personal study is not only a good way to teach others, but it also helps strengthen your understanding of what you have read.

Live by What You Learn

Scripture study should not only inspire us but also lead us to change the way we live. Listen to what the Spirit prompts you to do as you read, and then commit to act on those promptings.

President Russell M. Nelson said: "If we 'press forward, feasting upon the word of Christ, and endure to the end, . . . [we] shall have eternal life' [2 Nephi 31:20].

"To feast means more than to taste. To feast means to savor. We savor the scriptures by studying them in a spirit of delightful discovery and faithful obedience. When we feast upon the words of Christ, they are embedded 'in fleshy tables of the heart' [2 Corinthians 3:3]. They become an integral part of our nature" ("Living by Scriptural Guidance," *Ensign,* Nov. 2000, 17).

Ideas to Improve Your Family Scripture Study

Regular family scripture study is a powerful way to help your family learn the gospel. How much and how long you read as a family is not as important as being consistent in your efforts. As you make scripture study an important part of your family life, you will help your family members come closer to Jesus Christ and build their testimonies on the foundation of His word.

Consider the following questions:

- How can you encourage family members to study the scriptures on their own?

- What can you do to encourage family members to share what they are learning?

- How can you emphasize the principles you are learning in the Book of Mormon in everyday teaching moments?

Remember that the home is the ideal place for gospel learning. You can learn and teach the gospel at home in ways that are not possible in a Church class. Be creative as you think of ways to help your family learn from the scriptures. Consider some of the following ideas to enhance your family scripture study.

Use Music

Sing songs that reinforce the principles taught in the scriptures. Appendix D in this resource includes music related to the doctrines in each weekly outline.

Share Meaningful Scriptures

Give family members time to share scripture passages that they have found meaningful during their personal study.

Use Your Own Words

Invite family members to summarize in their own words what they learn from the scriptures you study.

Apply the Scriptures to Your Life

After reading a scripture passage, ask family members to share ways the passage applies to their lives.

Ask a Question

Invite family members to ask a gospel question, and then spend time looking for verses that can help answer the question.

Display a Scripture

Select a verse you find meaningful, and display it where family members will see it often. Invite other family members to take turns selecting a scripture to display.

Make a Scripture List

As a family, choose several verses that you would like to discuss during the coming week.

Memorize Scriptures

Select a scripture passage that is meaningful to your family, and invite family members to memorize it by repeating it daily or playing a memorization game.

Share Object Lessons

Find objects that relate to the chapters and verses that you are reading as a family. Invite family members to talk about how each object relates to the teachings in the scriptures.

Pick a Topic

Let family members take turns choosing a topic that the family will study together. Use the Topical Guide, the Bible Dictionary, or the Guide to the Scriptures (scriptures.ChurchofJesusChrist.org) to find scripture passages about the topic.

Draw a Picture

Read a few verses as a family, and then allow time for family members to draw something that relates to what you read. Spend time discussing one another's drawings.

Act Out a Story

After reading a story, invite family members to act it out. Afterward, talk about how the story relates to the things that you are experiencing individually and as a family.

Elder David A. Bednar taught: "Each family prayer, each episode of family scripture study, and each family home evening is a brushstroke on the canvas of our souls. No one event may appear to be very impressive or memorable. But just as the yellow and gold and brown strokes of paint complement each other and produce an impressive masterpiece, so our consistency in doing seemingly small things can lead to significant spiritual results" ("More Diligent and Concerned at Home," *Ensign* or *Liahona,* Nov. 2009, 19–20).

Additional Resources

All of these resources can be found in the Gospel Library app and on ChurchofJesusChrist.org.

Hymns and Children's Songbook

Sacred music invites the Spirit and teaches doctrine in a memorable way. In addition to the print versions of *Hymns* and *Children's Songbook,* you can find audio and video recordings of many hymns and children's songs at music.ChurchofJesusChrist.org and in the Sacred Music app.

Church Magazines

The *Friend, New Era, Ensign,* and *Liahona* magazines provide stories and activities that can supplement the principles you are teaching from *Come, Follow Me—For Individuals and Families.*

Book of Mormon Stories

Book of Mormon Stories can help children learn the doctrine and stories found in the Book of Mormon. You can also find videos of these stories in the Gospel Library app and at medialibrary.ChurchofJesusChrist.org.

Seminary and Institute Manuals

Seminary and institute manuals provide historical background and doctrinal commentary for principles and accounts found in the scriptures.

Media Library

Artwork, videos, and other media can help you and your family visualize the doctrine and stories found in the Book of Mormon. Visit medialibrary.ChurchofJesusChrist.org to browse the Church's collection of media resources, including the Book of Mormon video collection, which depicts events in the Book of Mormon. The Media Library is also available as a mobile app.

Gospel Topics

At topics.ChurchofJesusChrist.org you can find basic information about a variety of gospel topics, along with links to helpful resources, such as related general conference addresses, articles, scriptures, and videos. You can also find Gospel Topics Essays, which offer in-depth answers to gospel questions.

True to the Faith

If you need additional help understanding basic gospel principles, consider looking in *True to the Faith*. This resource consists of an alphabetical list of gospel topics explained in simple terms.

Teaching Young Children

If you have young children in your family, here are some activities that can help them learn:

- *Sing.* Hymns and songs from *Children's Songbook* teach doctrine powerfully. Use the topics index at the back of the *Children's Songbook* to find songs that relate to the gospel principles you are teaching. Help your children relate the messages of the songs to their lives. For example, you might ask questions about words or phrases in the lyrics. In addition to singing, your children can perform actions that go with the songs or listen to the songs as background music while they are doing other activities.

- *Listen to or act out a story.* Young children love stories—from the scriptures, from your life, from Church history, or from Church magazines. Look for ways to involve them in storytelling. They can hold pictures or objects, draw pictures of what they are hearing, act out the story, or even help tell the story. Help your children recognize the gospel truths in the stories you share.

- *Read a scripture.* Young children may not be able to read very much, but you can still engage them in learning from the scriptures. You may need to focus on a single verse, key phrase, or word. They may even be able to memorize short phrases from the scriptures if they repeat them a few times. As they hear the word of God, they will feel the Spirit.

- *Look at a picture or watch a video.* When you show your children a picture or video related to a gospel principle or scripture story, ask them questions that help them learn from what they are seeing. For example, you could ask, "What is happening in this picture or video? How does it make you feel?" The Gospel Library app, medialibrary.ChurchofJesusChrist.org, and children.ChurchofJesusChrist.org are good places to look for pictures and videos.

- *Create.* Children can build, draw, or color something related to the story or principle they are learning.

- *Participate in object lessons.* A simple object lesson can help your children understand a gospel principle that is difficult to comprehend. When using object lessons, find ways to let your children participate. They will learn more from an interactive experience than from just watching a demonstration.

- *Role-play.* When children role-play a situation they will likely encounter in real life, they are better able to understand how a gospel principle applies to their lives.

- *Repeat activities.* Young children may need to hear concepts multiple times to understand them. Don't be afraid to repeat stories or activities often. For example, you might share a scripture story several times in different ways—reading from the scriptures, summarizing in your own words, showing a video, letting your children help you tell the story, inviting them to act out the story, and so on.

Prophetic Promises

Studying the Book of Mormon will change you. It will change your family. Latter-day prophets have made promises about the power of the Book of Mormon since The Church of Jesus Christ of Latter-day Saints was restored. Ponder the following statements, and review them regularly. Which of these blessings would you like to receive? As you read the Book of Mormon, consider recording and sharing with others how these promises are fulfilled in your life.

The Prophet Joseph Smith: "I told the brethren that the Book of Mormon was the most correct of any book on earth, and the keystone of our religion, and a man would get nearer to God by abiding by its precepts, than by any other book" (*Teachings of Presidents of the Church: Joseph Smith* [2007], 64).

President Ezra Taft Benson: "It is not just that the Book of Mormon teaches us truth, though it indeed does that. It is not just that the Book of Mormon bears testimony of Christ, though it indeed does that, too. But there is something more. There is a power in the book which will begin to flow into your lives the moment you begin a serious study of the book. You will find greater power to resist temptation. You will find the power to avoid deception. You will find the power to stay on the strait and narrow path. The scriptures are called 'the words of life' (D&C 84:85), and nowhere is that more true than it is of the Book of Mormon. When you begin to hunger and thirst after those words, you will find life in greater and greater abundance" (*Teachings of Presidents of the Church: Ezra Taft Benson* [2014], 141).

President Gordon B. Hinckley: "Brothers and sisters, without reservation I promise you that if you will prayerfully read the Book of Mormon, regardless of how many times you previously have read it, there will come into your hearts an added measure of the Spirit of the Lord. There will come a strengthened resolution to walk in obedience to his commandments, and there will come a stronger testimony of the living reality of the Son of God" (*Teachings of Presidents of the Church: Gordon B. Hinckley* [2016], 233).

President Russell M. Nelson: "My dear brothers and sisters, I promise that as you prayerfully study the Book of Mormon *every day,* you will make better decisions—*every day.* I promise that as you ponder what you study, the windows of heaven will open, and you will receive answers to your own questions and direction for your own life. I promise that as you daily immerse yourself in the Book of Mormon, you can be immunized against the evils of the day, even the gripping plague of pornography and other mind-numbing addictions" ("The Book of Mormon: What Would Your Life Be Like without It?" *Ensign* or *Liahona,* Nov. 2017, 62–63).

Portrait of Christ the Savior, by Heinrich Hofmann

Introductory Pages of the Book of Mormon

"ANOTHER TESTAMENT OF JESUS CHRIST"

Your study of the Book of Mormon can be enriched if you start by reading the pages that precede 1 Nephi. What do you find that strengthens your testimony?

RECORD YOUR IMPRESSIONS

Before you even get to 1 Nephi chapter 1, it's clear that the Book of Mormon is no ordinary book. Its introductory pages describe a backstory unlike any other—including visits of angels, an ancient record buried for centuries in a hillside, and an obscure farmer translating the record by the power of God. The Book of Mormon is not just a history of ancient American civilizations. It contains "the fulness of the everlasting gospel" (introduction to the Book of Mormon), and God Himself directed its coming forth—how it was written, how it was preserved, and how it was made available in our day. This year, as you read the Book of Mormon, pray about it, and apply its teachings, you will invite its power into your life, and you may feel to say, as the Three Witnesses did in their testimony, "It is marvelous in [my] eyes."

Ideas for Personal Scripture Study

TITLE PAGE OF THE BOOK OF MORMON

The Book of Mormon can strengthen my faith in Jesus Christ.

The title page of the Book of Mormon provides more than just a title. Among other things, it lists several purposes of this sacred record. Look for these purposes, and then as you study the Book of Mormon this year, note passages that you feel accomplish these purposes. For example, what passages help convince you "that Jesus is the Christ, the Eternal God"?

INTRODUCTION TO THE BOOK OF MORMON

The Book of Mormon "outlines the plan of salvation."

The plan of salvation is Heavenly Father's plan to help His children become exalted, as He is, and experience the joy He feels (see 2 Nephi 2:25–26). The Atonement of Jesus Christ makes this plan possible, and every doctrine, ordinance, covenant, and commandment that God has given is meant to help accomplish the plan.

If you want to understand the plan of salvation, there's no better book to read than the Book of Mormon. It refers to God's plan—using a variety of names—more than 20 times. During your study this year, notice when God's plan is mentioned or alluded to and what the Book of Mormon says about it.

Here's an activity to get you started. Read the following passages, and list the different names given to God's plan: 2 Nephi 9:13; 11:5; and Alma 12:32–34; 24:14; 41:2; 42:15–16. What do each of these names suggest to you about the Father's plan?

"THE TESTIMONY OF THREE WITNESSES"; "THE TESTIMONY OF EIGHT WITNESSES"

I can be a witness of the Book of Mormon.

The Holy Ghost can testify to you that the Book of Mormon is true, even if you haven't seen the golden plates as the Three Witnesses and Eight Witnesses did. How do their testimonies strengthen yours? How can you "give [your name] unto the world, to witness unto the world" what you know about the Book of Mormon? ("The Testimony of Eight Witnesses").

"THE TESTIMONY OF THE PROPHET JOSEPH SMITH"

The coming forth of the Book of Mormon was a miracle.

If someone asked you where the Book of Mormon came from, what would you say? How would you describe the Lord's hand in bringing forth the Book of Mormon? How did Joseph Smith describe the coming forth of the Book of Mormon?

"THE TESTIMONY OF THE PROPHET JOSEPH SMITH"

How was the Book of Mormon translated?

The Book of Mormon was translated "by the gift and power of God." We don't know many details about the miraculous translation process, but we do know that Joseph Smith was a seer, aided by instruments that God had prepared: two transparent stones called the Urim and Thummim and another stone called a seer stone. Joseph saw in these stones the English interpretation of the characters on the plates, and he read the translation aloud while a scribe recorded it. Each of Joseph's scribes testified that God's power was manifest in the translation of this sacred work.

See "Book of Mormon Translation," Gospel Topics, topics.ChurchofJesusChrist.org.

Ideas for Family Scripture Study and Family Home Evening

As you read the scriptures with your family, the Spirit can help you know what principles to emphasize and discuss in order to meet the needs of your family. Here are some ideas.

Title page of the Book of Mormon. Perhaps your family could start a list of verses from the Book of Mormon that have built your faith "that Jesus is the Christ" and add to it throughout the year. This might also be a good time to create a family plan for reading the Book of Mormon: When and where will you gather to read? How will each family member participate? For additional help, see "Ideas to Improve Your Family Scripture Study" at the beginning of this resource.

The Book of Mormon is the keystone of our religion.

Introduction to the Book of Mormon. A keystone is a wedge-shaped stone at the top of an arch that locks the other stones together. To help your family understand how the Book of Mormon is "the keystone of our religion," you could build or draw an arch with a keystone at the top. What happens if the keystone is removed? What would happen if we did not have the Book of Mormon? How can we make the Book of Mormon the keystone of our faith in Jesus Christ?

"The Testimony of Three Witnesses"; "The Testimony of Eight Witnesses." Your family members could write down their own testimonies about the Book of Mormon, sign their names on them, and think of ways to share their testimonies with others.

"The Testimony of the Prophet Joseph Smith." In Joseph Smith's account, what evidence do we find that God was involved in the bringing forth of the Book of Mormon?

For more ideas for teaching children, see this week's outline in *Come, Follow Me—For Primary.*

Improving Personal Study

A prophetic promise. President Russell M. Nelson said, "I promise that as you ponder what you study [in the Book of Mormon], the windows of heaven will open, and you will receive answers to your own questions and direction for your own life" ("The Book of Mormon: What Would Your Life Be Like without It?" *Ensign* or *Liahona,* Nov. 2017, 62–63).

Moroni Delivers the Golden Plates, by Gary L. Kapp

Lehi Traveling Near the Red Sea, by Gary Smith

1 Nephi 1–7

"I WILL GO AND DO"

Nephi recorded the "things of God" (1 Nephi 6:3). As you study Nephi's record, pay attention to the things of God you find, especially impressions from the Spirit.

RECORD YOUR IMPRESSIONS_____

_____

_____

The Book of Mormon begins with an account of a real family experiencing real struggles. It happened in 600 BC, but there are things about this account that might sound familiar to families today. This family was living in a world of increasing wickedness, but the Lord promised them that if they would follow Him, He would lead them to safety. Along the way they had good moments and bad moments; they experienced great blessings and miracles, but they also had their fair share of arguments and contention. Rarely in scripture is there such a lengthy account of a family trying to live the gospel: a father struggling to inspire faith in his family, sons deciding whether they will believe him, a mother fearing for the safety of her children, and brothers dealing with jealousy and contention—and sometimes forgiving each other. Overall, there is real power in following the examples of faith that this family—despite their imperfections—demonstrated.

Ideas for Personal Scripture Study

The scriptures are of great worth.

The first six chapters of the Book of Mormon contain many references to sacred books, sacred records, and the word of the Lord. As you read 1 Nephi 1–6, what do you learn about why the word of God is "of great worth"? (1 Nephi 5:21). What do these passages teach you about the scriptures? What do you find that inspires you to search the scriptures with greater commitment?

See also "Scriptures Legacy" (video, ChurchofJesusChrist.org).

The Book of Mormon testifies of Jesus Christ.

True to the purpose stated on its title page—to convince all that Jesus is the Christ—the Book of Mormon opens with Lehi's remarkable vision of the Savior. What do you learn about Jesus Christ from what Lehi saw? What are some of the Savior's "great and marvelous" works in your life? (1 Nephi 1:14).

When I seek and trust the Lord, He can soften my heart.

Although Laman, Lemuel, and Nephi all grew up in the same family and had similar experiences, there is quite a contrast between the ways they responded to the divine direction their father received in this chapter. As you read 1 Nephi 2, see if you can identify why Nephi's heart was softened while his brothers' hearts were not. You might also think about your own responses to direction from the Lord, whether through the Holy Ghost or His prophet. When have you felt the Lord soften your heart so you could more willingly accept His direction and counsel?

God will prepare a way for me to do His will.

When the Lord commanded Lehi and his family to obtain the plates of brass from Laban, He did not give specific instructions on how to accomplish this commandment. This is often true of other commandments or personal revelations we receive from God, and this might lead us to feel like He has required "a hard thing" (1 Nephi 3:5). What inspires you about Nephi's response to the Lord's command, found in 1 Nephi 3:7, 15–16? Is there anything you feel impressed to "go and do"?

As you study 1 Nephi 1–7, look for ways God prepared the way for Lehi and his family. How has He done this for you?

See also Proverbs 3:5–6; 1 Nephi 17:3; "Obedience," Gospel Topics, topics.ChurchofJesusChrist.org; Book of Mormon Videos collection on ChurchofJesusChrist.org or the Gospel Library app.

Remembering the works of God can give me the faith to obey His commandments.

When Laman and Lemuel felt like murmuring, they usually had Nephi and Lehi nearby to encourage and admonish them. When you feel like murmuring, reading the words of Nephi and Lehi can provide valuable counsel and perspective. How did Nephi and Lehi try to help their family members build faith in God? (see 1 Nephi 4:1–3; 5:1–8; 7:6–21). What do you learn from their examples that can help you next time you are tempted to murmur or rebel?

Ideas for Family Scripture Study and Family Home Evening

As you read the scriptures with your family, the Spirit can help you know what principles to emphasize and discuss in order to meet the needs of your family. Here are some ideas.

Nephi and his family valued the words of the prophets.

1 Nephi 1–7. Throughout 1 Nephi 1–7, you could encourage family members to notice interactions between members of Lehi and Sariah's family. What can we learn from these relationships that can help our family?

1 Nephi 2:20. The principle in 1 Nephi 2:20 is repeated often throughout the Book of Mormon. How can your family members apply it to their lives as you study the Book of Mormon together this year? Perhaps you could make a poster together featuring the Lord's promise in this verse and display it in your home. It could serve as a reminder to periodically discuss how you have seen the Lord

prosper your family when you have kept His commandments. Consider noting these experiences on the poster.

1 Nephi 2:11–13; 3:5–7. Perhaps your family would benefit from noting the difference between Laman and Lemuel's response to the Lord's commands and Nephi's response. What can we learn from 1 Nephi 2:11–13; 3:5–7 about murmuring? What blessings come when we exercise faith?

1 Nephi 3:19–20; 5:10–22; 6. These verses could inspire your family to keep a record of important events and experiences from your lives. Maybe you could start a family journal, similar to the records Nephi and Lehi kept about their family's experiences. What might you include in your family record?

1 Nephi 7:19–21. What impresses us about Nephi's example in these verses? How is our family blessed when we "frankly forgive" each other?

For more ideas for teaching children, see this week's outline in *Come, Follow Me—For Primary.*

Improving Our Teaching

Study the scriptures consistently. One key to meaningful teaching in the home is to create consistent learning opportunities for your family. President Thomas S. Monson taught, "Crash courses are not nearly so effective as the day-to-day reading and application of the scriptures in our lives" ("Be Your Best Self," *Ensign* or *Liahona*, May 2009, 68).

I Did Obey the Voice of the Spirit, by Walter Rane

Lehi's Dream, by Steven Lloyd Neal

1 Nephi 8–10

"COME AND PARTAKE OF THE FRUIT"

As you read 1 Nephi 8–10, consider what messages from Lehi's vision apply to you. Record the spiritual impressions you receive in your scriptures, a notebook, or this resource.

RECORD YOUR IMPRESSIONS

Lehi's dream—with its iron rod, mists of darkness, spacious building, and tree with "most sweet" fruit— is an inspiring invitation to receive the blessings of the Savior's love and atoning sacrifice. For Lehi, however, this vision was also about his family: "Because of the thing which I have seen, I have reason to rejoice in the Lord because of Nephi and also of Sam. . . . But behold, Laman and Lemuel, I fear exceedingly because of you" (1 Nephi 8:3–4). When Lehi finished describing his vision, he pleaded with Laman and Lemuel to "hearken to his words, that perhaps the Lord would be merciful to them" (1 Nephi 8:37). Even if you have studied Lehi's vision many times, this time think about it the way Lehi did—think of someone you love. As you do, the security of the iron rod, the dangers of the spacious building, and the sweetness of the fruit will take on new meaning. And you will understand more deeply "all the feeling of [the] tender parent" who received this remarkable vision.

Ideas for Personal Scripture Study

1 NEPHI 8

The word of God leads me to the Savior and helps me feel His love.

Lehi's vision offers an invitation to reflect on where you are—and where you are going—in your personal journey to know the Savior and feel His love. President Boyd K. Packer taught: "You may think that Lehi's dream or vision has no special meaning for you, but it does. You are in it; all of us are in it (see 1 Nephi 19:23). Lehi's dream or vision of the iron rod has in it everything a . . . Latter-day Saint needs to understand the test of life" ("Lehi's Dream and You," *New Era,* Jan. 2015, 2).

Lehi eating the fruit of the tree of life. *Tree of Life,* by Marcus Alan Vincent

One way to study 1 Nephi 8 could be to fill out a chart like the one shown here. To understand the meaning of the symbols, it is helpful to refer to the vision that Nephi had when he prayed to understand his father's vision—see especially 1 Nephi 11:4–25, 32–36; 12:16–18; and 15:21–33, 36. As you study Lehi's vision, consider what the Lord wants you to learn.

Symbol from Lehi's vision	Meanings	Questions to ponder
Tree and its fruit (1 Nephi 8:10–12)		What am I doing to invite others to partake of the love of God?
River (1 Nephi 8:13)		
Rod of iron (1 Nephi 8:19–20, 30)		
Mist of darkness (1 Nephi 8:23)		
Great and spacious build-ing (1 Nephi 8:26–27, 33)		

See also David A. Bednar, "Lehi's Dream: Holding Fast to the Rod," *Ensign* or *Liahona,* Oct. 2011, 33–37.

1 NEPHI 9

Why did Nephi make two sets of plates?

The Lord's "wise purpose" in having Nephi create two records became clear centuries later. After Joseph Smith translated the first 116 manuscript pages of the Book of Mormon, he gave the pages to Martin Harris, who lost them (see D&C 10:1–23). But Nephi's second set of plates covered the same time period, and the Lord commanded Joseph Smith to translate these plates rather than retranslate what had been lost (see D&C 10:38–45).

For more about the plates mentioned in 1 Nephi 9, see "A Brief Explanation about the Book of Mormon"; 1 Nephi 19:1–5; 2 Nephi 5:29–32; and Words of Mormon 1:3–9.

1 NEPHI 10:2–16

Ancient prophets knew about Jesus Christ's mission and testified of Him.

The account of Lehi's vision surely made an impression on his family, but he still had other eternal truths to teach them about the Savior's mission. As you read 1 Nephi 10:2–16, think about why the Lord would want Lehi's family—and all of us—to know these truths. Consider what you could tell your loved ones to invite them to turn to the Savior. After studying Lehi's vision and teachings, what are you, like Nephi, inspired to learn "by the power of the Holy Ghost"? (1 Nephi 10:17).

1 NEPHI 10:17–19

God will reveal truth to me if I diligently seek it.

How do you respond when you encounter a gospel principle that you don't understand? Note the differences between the way Nephi responded to Lehi's vision (see 1 Nephi 10:17–19; 11:1) and the way Laman and Lemuel responded (see 1 Nephi 15:1–10). Why did they respond in these ways, and what were the results of their responses?

Consider writing about a time when you wanted to know if a gospel teaching was true. How did the process you followed compare with what Nephi did?

See also 1 Nephi 2:11–19; Doctrine and Covenants 8:1–3.

Ideas for Family Scripture Study and Family Home Evening

As you read the scriptures with your family, the Spirit can help you know what principles to emphasize and discuss in order to meet the needs of your family. Here are some ideas.

1 Nephi 8. Your family members might enjoy reenacting Lehi's vision or drawing pictures and using their drawings to tell about it. Or you could show the artist's depiction of Lehi's vision that accompanies this lesson and invite family members to point out details and look for scriptures that describe what these things represent. The hymn "The Iron Rod" (*Hymns,* no. 274) goes well with this chapter. You might also watch a video depicting Lehi's vision (see the Book of Mormon Videos collection on ChurchofJesusChrist.org or the Gospel Library app).

1 Nephi 8:10–16. Who could we invite to come closer to Jesus Christ and feel the sweetness of His love? What can we do to "[beckon] unto them"?

1 Nephi 9:5–6. When have we followed a commandment without fully understanding the reasons for it? How were we blessed?

1 Nephi 10:20–22. How is being physically unclean similar to being spiritually unclean? What can we do to make sure we are remaining spiritually clean?

For more ideas for teaching children, see this week's outline in *Come, Follow Me—For Primary.*

Improving Our Teaching

How do the scriptures apply to our lives? After reading a passage of scripture, invite family members to share how the passage applies to them. For instance, when your family members read 1 Nephi 8:33, they might talk about how to give no heed to those who "point the finger of scorn."

The Tree of Life, by Avon Oakeson

Sweeter Than All Sweetness, by Miguel Angel González Romero

1 Nephi 11–15

"ARMED WITH RIGHTEOUSNESS AND WITH THE POWER OF GOD"

Can you see yourself in 1 Nephi 11–15? What passages are of most value to you and your family?

RECORD YOUR IMPRESSIONS

When God has a monumental work for His prophet to do, He often gives that prophet a monumental vision that helps him understand God's purposes for His children. Moses saw a vision of "this earth, and the inhabitants thereof, and also the heavens" (Moses 1:36). The Apostle John saw the history of the world and the Savior's Second Coming (see the book of Revelation). Joseph Smith saw the Father and the Son (see Joseph Smith—History 1:17–18). Lehi saw a vision that portrayed the journey we must make toward the Savior and His love.

As recorded in 1 Nephi 11–14, Nephi saw the ministry of the Savior, the future of Lehi's posterity in the promised land, and the latter-day destiny of God's work. This vision helped to prepare Nephi for the work that lay ahead of him, and it can also help prepare you—for God has a work for you to do in His kingdom. You are among "the saints of the church of the Lamb" seen by Nephi, "who were scattered upon all the face of the earth; and they were armed with righteousness and with the power of God in great glory" (1 Nephi 14:14).

Ideas for Personal Scripture Study

1 NEPHI 11

God sent Jesus Christ as an expression of His love.

To help Nephi understand the meaning of the tree that his father had seen, an angel showed him "the Son of the Eternal Father" (1 Nephi 11:21). This led Nephi to conclude that the tree represents the love of God. But the vision wasn't over yet. As you read and ponder 1 Nephi 11, what do you find that helps you understand why Jesus Christ is the ultimate expression of God's love?

To learn about other symbols in Lehi's dream, see 1 Nephi 11:35–36; 12:16–18; and 15:21–30.

See also John 3:16.

1 NEPHI 12–13

The Lord prepared the way for the Restoration.

Nephi would never live to witness much of what he saw in his vision. Why do you think it was valuable for Nephi to know these things? Why is it valuable for *you* to know these things? Maybe you could ask this question each time you read about something Nephi saw in his vision.

Here are some of the events Nephi saw: the future of his people (see chapter 12), the colonizing of the Americas and the American Revolution (see chapter 13:12–19), the Great Apostasy (see chapter 13:20–29), and the Restoration of the gospel (see chapter 13:32–42).

1 NEPHI 13:1–9; 14:9–11

What is the "great and abominable church" that Nephi saw?

Elder Dallin H. Oaks explained that the "great and abominable church" described by Nephi represents "any philosophy or organization that opposes belief in God. And the 'captivity' into which this 'church' seeks to bring the saints will not be so much physical confinement as the captivity of false ideas" ("Stand as Witnesses of God," *Ensign,* Mar. 2015, 32).

1 NEPHI 13:12

Who was the man Nephi saw whom the Spirit "wrought upon" to go "forth upon the many waters"?

Nephi saw that the Holy Ghost would inspire Christopher Columbus to make his famous voyage to the Americas. On March 14, 1493, Columbus wrote of this voyage: "These great and marvelous results are not to be attributed to any merit of mine . . . ; for that which the unaided intellect of man could not compass, the Spirit of God has granted to human exertions, for God is wont to hear the prayers of His servants who love His precepts even to the performance of apparent impossibilities" (*The Annals of America* [Encyclopedia Britannica, Inc., 1976], 1:5).

1 NEPHI 13:20–42

Latter-day scripture restores "plain and precious things."

Nephi saw in vision that the Bible—which he described as "a record of the Jews"—would have "many plain and precious things taken away from [it]" (1 Nephi 13:23, 28). However, he also saw that God would restore these things through "other books"—the Book of Mormon and other latter-day scripture (see 1 Nephi 13:39–40). What are some of the precious truths that the Book of Mormon helps us better understand? How is your life different because these plain and precious things have been restored?

The Book of Mormon restores gospel truths lost during the Apostasy.

See also "Plain and Precious Truths," *Ensign,* Mar. 2008, 68–73; Russell M. Nelson, "The Book of Mormon: What Would Your Life Be Like without It?" *Ensign* or *Liahona,* Nov. 2017, 60–63.

1 NEPHI 15:1–11

The Lord will answer me if I ask in faith with a soft heart.

Have you ever felt like you weren't receiving personal revelation—that God wasn't talking to you? What counsel did Nephi give his brothers when they felt this way? How can you apply Nephi's counsel in your life, and how can you use his counsel to help others?

See also Jacob 4:8; Alma 5:46; 26:21–22.

Ideas for Family Scripture Study and Family Home Evening

As you read the scriptures with your family, the Spirit can help you know what principles to emphasize and discuss in order to meet the needs of your family. Here are some ideas.

1 Nephi 11–14. As your family reads these chapters, occasionally stop and ask questions like these: What did Nephi see in his vision that might have made him happy? What might have made him sad? Why?

1 Nephi 13:20–42. To help family members understand the value of the "plain and precious" truths in the Book of Mormon, compare a clearly written message to a scrambled message. Why might Heavenly Father want His truths to be taught clearly? Family members might bear testimony of some "plain and precious" truths they have learned from the Book of Mormon.

1 Nephi 14:12–15. Why are we "armed with righteousness and with the power of God" when we live true to our covenants with God?

1 Nephi 15:8–11. What experiences can your family share when they have "inquired of the Lord"? What do we learn from Nephi's example?

For more ideas for teaching children, see this week's outline in *Come, Follow Me—For Primary.*

Improving Personal Study

Use study helps. The footnotes, the Topical Guide, and other study helps provide insights into the scriptures. For example, what do the footnotes help you understand about 1 Nephi 14:20–21?

Nephi's Vision of Mary, by James Johnson

Lehi and the Liahona, by Joseph Brickey

1 Nephi 16–22

"I WILL PREPARE THE WAY BEFORE YOU"

As you study 1 Nephi 16–22, look for passages that impress you. Some people like to highlight such verses in their scriptures; others write notes in the margins. Consider how you will record the impressions you receive.

RECORD YOUR IMPRESSIONS

As Lehi's family journeyed toward the promised land, the Lord made them this promise: "I will prepare the way before you, if it so be that ye shall keep my commandments" (1 Nephi 17:13). Clearly, that promise did not mean that the journey would be easy—family members still disagreed, bows broke, and people struggled and died, and they still had to build a ship from raw materials. However, when the family faced adversity or seemingly impossible tasks,

Nephi recognized that the Lord was never far away. He knew that God "doth nourish [the faithful], and strengthen them, and provide means whereby they can accomplish the thing which he has commanded them" (1 Nephi 17:3). If you ever wonder why bad things happen to good people like Nephi and his family, you may find insights in these chapters. But perhaps more important, you will see what good people *do* when bad things happen.

Ideas for Personal Scripture Study

1 NEPHI 16–18

When I keep the commandments, God will help me face challenges.

Chapters 16–18 of 1 Nephi describe several challenges that Nephi's family faced, including dealing with a broken bow (see 1 Nephi 16:17–32), the death of Ishmael (see 1 Nephi 16:34–39), building a ship (see 1 Nephi 17:7–16; 18:1–4), and family discord (see 1 Nephi 18:9–22). How did Nephi's responses to these challenges differ from the responses of some of his family members? What were the consequences of these responses?

It might help to record what you find in a table with headings like these: "Challenge," "Nephi's Response," "Others' Responses," and "Results." Why do you think Nephi was able to remain so faithful when others did not? Reflect on how the example of Nephi and his family can help you with your challenges.

See also related videos in the Book of Mormon Videos collection on ChurchofJesusChrist.org or the Gospel Library app.

1 NEPHI 16:10–16, 23–31; 18:11–22

The Lord guides me through small and simple means.

When God led Lehi's family into the wilderness, He did not provide them with a detailed travel plan to the promised land. But He did give Lehi the Liahona to guide his family daily toward their destination. What has Heavenly Father given you to provide guidance and direction? What do you

think it means that "by small means the Lord can bring about great things"? (1 Nephi 16:29).

As you read 1 Nephi 16:10–16, 23–31 and 18:11–22, consider making a list of principles that illustrate how God guides His children (for example, 1 Nephi 16:10 can teach that God sometimes guides us in unexpected ways). What experiences have you had with these principles?

See also Alma 37:7, 38–47; Doctrine and Covenants 64:33–34.

If Ye Are Prepared Ye Shall Not Fear, by Clark Kelley Price

1 NEPHI 19:23–24; 20–22

I can "liken all scriptures" to myself.

Isaiah wrote to all the children of Israel, and Nephi saw that this included his own family specifically—and it includes you (see 1 Nephi 19:23–24). Regarding Nephi's quotations of Isaiah, President Henry B. Eyring said, "I read Isaiah's words . . . assuming Nephi picked the parts of Isaiah that I, without worrying about the imagery, could take directly to my heart as if the Lord were speaking to me" ("The Book of Mormon Will Change Your Life," *Ensign,* Feb. 2004, 10).

With President Eyring's words in mind, consider questions like the following as you read chapters 20–22:

1 Nephi 20:1–9. What phrases in these verses describe the children of Israel? How do they describe Laman and Lemuel? What warnings and application do you find for yourself?

1 Nephi 20:17–22. How did the Lord lead the children of Israel? How did He lead Lehi's family? How does He guide you?

What else do you find in 1 Nephi 20–22 that makes you feel as if the Lord were speaking to you? How does Nephi's commentary in chapter 22 help you understand Isaiah's prophecies?

1 NEPHI 21

Who are the house of Israel and the Gentiles?

The house of Israel are the descendants of the Old Testament prophet Jacob, who was given the name Israel by the Lord (see Genesis 32:28; 35:10; see also Bible Dictionary, "Israel"). The Lord made certain covenants with Israel, and his descendants were considered God's covenant people. However, generations later, many of them turned away from the Lord and were eventually scattered across the earth.

The term *Gentiles* in these passages refers to people that do not yet have the gospel (see Bible Dictionary, "Gentile"). Isaiah taught that in the latter days the Gentiles would be given the gospel and be instrumental in teaching and gathering the house of Israel (see 1 Nephi 21:22; 22:8–12; see also Isaiah 60; 66:18–20).

Ideas for Family Scripture Study and Family Home Evening

As you read the scriptures with your family, the Spirit can help you know what principles to emphasize and discuss in order to meet the needs of your family. Here are some ideas.

1 Nephi 17:1–6, 17–22. Perhaps your family could contrast Nephi's account of traveling in the wilderness (see 1 Nephi 17:1–6) with his brothers' account (see 1 Nephi 17:17–22). Why do you think they saw the same events so differently? What can we learn from Nephi about having a faithful perspective?

1 Nephi 17:17–22; 18:9–16. What are the consequences of jealousy, contention, and complaining in a family? How can we overcome these problems?

1 Nephi 19:22–24. Nephi likened the scriptures to his family "that it might be for [their] profit and learning" (1 Nephi 19:23). There are several stories in 1 Nephi 16–18 that your family could liken to yourselves. Maybe you could act out one of these stories and discuss how it applies to your family.

1 Nephi 21:14–16. How might the message in these verses help someone who feels forgotten?

For more ideas for teaching children, see this week's outline in *Come, Follow Me—For Primary*.

Improving Personal Study

Ask the Lord for help. The scriptures were given by revelation, and we need revelation to truly understand them. The Lord has promised, "If ye will . . . ask me in faith, . . . surely these things shall be made known unto you" (1 Nephi 15:11).

They Did Treat Me with Much Harshness, by Walter Rane

Adam and Eve, by Douglas Fryer

2 Nephi 1–5

"WE LIVED AFTER THE MANNER OF HAPPINESS"

The scriptures can open the door to personal revelation. As you read 2 Nephi 1–5, you may find that the Lord has something specific that He wants to teach you.

RECORD YOUR IMPRESSIONS _____

_____

_____

If you knew your life was coming to an end, what final messages would you want to share with those you love most? When the prophet Lehi felt he was nearing the end of his life, he gathered his children together one last time to prophesy and share the gospel truths he cherished with the people he cherished. He taught of liberty, obedience, the Fall of Adam and Eve, redemption through Jesus Christ, and joy. Not all of his children accepted his final testimony, but those who did—along with the millions who read it today—found in his testimony principles for living "after the manner of happiness" (2 Nephi 5:27).

Ideas for Personal Scripture Study

2 NEPHI 2

I am free to choose eternal life.

Elder D. Todd Christofferson said: "God intends that His children should act according to the moral agency He has given them. . . . It is His plan and His will that we have the principal decision-making role in our own life's drama" ("Free Forever, to Act for Themselves," *Ensign* or *Liahona,* Nov. 2014, 16). In his teachings about agency, Lehi identified essential conditions that make agency possible and enable us to reach our divine potential, including the following:

1. A knowledge of good and evil (2 Nephi 2:5)

2. A law given to mankind (2 Nephi 2:5)

3. Opposing, enticing choices (2 Nephi 2:11)

4. Power to act (2 Nephi 2:16)

As you read 2 Nephi 2, what do you learn about each of these conditions of agency and their relationship to each other? What would happen to our agency if one or more of these conditions were missing? What else do you learn about agency from Lehi's words?

2 NEPHI 2:22–29

The Fall and the Atonement of Jesus Christ are essential parts of Heavenly Father's plan.

Many people see the Fall of Adam and Eve as a tragic event. However, Lehi's teachings about the Fall reveal why it was a necessary part of the Father's plan for our eternal progression. As you read these verses, look for why the Fall needed to happen in order for us—Heavenly Father's children—to progress. How did the Savior's atoning sacrifice redeem us from the Fall?

See also Moses 5:9–12; 6:51–62; "Fall of Adam and Eve," Gospel Topics, topics.ChurchofJesusChrist.org.

2 NEPHI 3:6–24

Joseph Smith was foreordained to restore the gospel.

The last part of 2 Nephi 3 contains a prophecy given by Joseph of Egypt about a future seer who would share his name (see verses 14–15)—Joseph Smith. It also has a lot to say about Joseph Smith's mission.

What do verses 6–24 say that Joseph Smith, a "choice seer," would do to bless God's people? How has Joseph Smith's work been "of great worth" to you?

One important part of Joseph Smith's mission was to bring forth the writings of the seed of Joseph, which are contained in the Book of Mormon. What do you learn from this chapter about the importance of the Book of Mormon?

See also Joseph Smith Translation, Genesis 50:24–38 (in Bible appendix).

Prophet of the Lord, by David Lindsley

2 NEPHI 4:15–35

I can turn to God in my weakness.

Nephi had recently lost his father. The responsibility for leading his family now rested on him. He felt surrounded by temptation and was discouraged because of his sins. Even if your circumstances are different from Nephi's, you may relate to some of his thoughts and emotions recorded in 2 Nephi 4:15–35. What helped Nephi in his afflictions? How can Nephi's response to his challenges help you face your struggles?

2 NEPHI 5

Happiness is found in living the gospel.

How would you define happiness? Nephi wrote that his people lived "after the manner of happiness" (2 Nephi 5:27). You might look for choices Nephi and his people made that led to happiness—ways they supported each other and their families, what they valued in their community, and so on. What do you learn that can help you build a life of happiness, as the people of Nephi did?

2 NEPHI 5:20–21

What is the "curse" that came upon the Lamanites?

"The dark skin was placed upon the Lamanites so that they could be distinguished from the Nephites and to keep the two peoples from mixing [see 2 Nephi 5:21–23; Alma 3:6–10]. The dark skin was the sign of the curse. The curse was the withdrawal of the Spirit of the Lord [see 2 Nephi 5:20]. . . . Dark skin . . . is no longer to be considered a sign of the curse" (Joseph Fielding Smith, *Answers to Gospel Questions,* comp. Joseph Fielding Smith Jr. [1960], 3:122–23).

Ideas for Family Scripture Study and Family Home Evening

As you read the scriptures with your family, the Spirit will help you know what principles to emphasize and discuss in order to meet the needs of your family. Here are some ideas.

2 Nephi 1:13–25. What do these verses teach us about a righteous parent's greatest wishes for his or her children?

2 Nephi 3:6. Read together "Seer" in the Bible Dictionary. How was Joseph Smith a seer? Why are we grateful for the work that Joseph Smith accomplished? (see 2 Nephi 3:6–24).

2 Nephi 4:20–25. As you read 2 Nephi 4:20–25 together, pause after each verse, and invite family members to share when they have experienced or felt what Nephi describes. What has God done for our family?

2 Nephi 5. What are some of the ways your family is living "after the manner of happiness"? As your family reads 2 Nephi 5, you could discuss the things the Nephites cared about: family (verse 6), the commandments (verse 10), the scriptures (verse 12), education (verse 15), temples (verse 16), work (verse 17), and Church callings (verse 26). One way to do this is to find objects that represent some of these things and talk about how we show that we, like the Nephites, value these same things.

For more ideas for teaching children, see this week's outline in *Come, Follow Me—For Primary.*

Improving Our Teaching

Be observant. If you pay attention to what is happening in your children's lives, you will find excellent teaching opportunities. Comments your children make or questions they ask can also be opportunities for teaching moments. (See *Teaching in the Savior's Way,* 16.)

Lehi and His People Arrive in the New World, by Clark Kelley Price

Not My Will, But Thine, Be Done, by Harry Anderson

FEBRUARY 10–16

2 Nephi 6–10

"O HOW GREAT THE PLAN OF OUR GOD!"

As you read 2 Nephi 6–10, ponder what the Lord is trying to teach you. As you identify these truths, record them and prayerfully consider how you can act on what you are learning.

RECORD YOUR IMPRESSIONS

It had been at least 40 years since Lehi's family left Jerusalem. They were in a strange new land, half a world away from Jerusalem and the rest of God's covenant people. Lehi had died, and his posterity had already started what would become a centuries-long contention between the Nephites—"who believed in the warnings and the revelations of God"—and the Lamanites, who did not (2 Nephi 5:6). In these circumstances, Jacob, who was Nephi's younger brother and now ordained as a teacher for the Nephites, wanted the

covenant people to know that God would never forget them, so they must never forget Him. This is a message we surely need in our own world, where covenants are belittled and revelation rejected. "Let us remember him, . . . for we are not cast off. . . . Great are the promises of the Lord," he declared (2 Nephi 10:20–21). Among those promises, none is greater than the promise of an "infinite atonement" to overcome death and hell (2 Nephi 9:7). "Therefore," Jacob concluded, "cheer up your hearts"! (2 Nephi 10:23).

Ideas for Personal Scripture Study

2 NEPHI 6-8

The Lord is merciful to His people and will fulfill His promises.

To help his people understand that they were part of the house of Israel and could trust God and His promises, Jacob quoted prophecies of Isaiah, recorded in 2 Nephi 6–8. Isaiah described the scattering of Israel and the Savior's promised gathering and redemption of His people. As you read, ponder questions like the following:

- What do I learn about the Savior's redeeming love for me?

- What comfort does the Savior offer to those who seek Him?

- What can I do to more faithfully "wait" for the Savior and His promised blessings?

2 NEPHI 9:1-26

Through His Atonement, Jesus Christ delivers all people from physical and spiritual death.

What words or images would you use to communicate to someone our desperate need for a Redeemer to rescue us from death and sin? Jacob used the words "awful" and "monster." What did Jacob teach about "that monster, death and hell" and the "escape" that God has prepared for us? (2 Nephi 9:10). As you read 2 Nephi 9:1–26, consider marking in one color what would happen to us without the Atonement of Jesus Christ. Then, in another color, you could mark what we can receive through the Savior's Atonement.

What truths do you find about the Atonement of Jesus Christ that cause you to praise the "wisdom of God, his mercy and grace"? (2 Nephi 9:8).

See also "Atonement of Jesus Christ," Gospel Topics, topics.ChurchofJesusChrist.org.

2 NEPHI 9:27-54

I can come unto Christ and receive the glorious blessings of His Atonement.

Jesus Christ came "into the world that he may save all men *if* they will hearken unto his voice" (2 Nephi 9:21; italics added). In other words, we must be willing to accept the saving blessings He offers. After describing the great plan of redemption, Jacob gave important warnings and invitations, found in 2 Nephi 9:27–54, to help us receive the blessings of the Atonement. Consider recording them on a chart like this one:

Warnings	Invitations

What do you feel prompted by the Spirit to do in response to these warnings and invitations?

2 NEPHI 10:20, 23-25

Because of the sacrifice of Jesus Christ, I can "cheer up" my heart.

Jacob's message was a joyful one. "I speak unto you these things," he said, "that ye may rejoice, and lift up your heads forever" (2 Nephi 9:3). As you read 2 Nephi 10:20, 23–25, what do you find that gives you hope? What else have you found in 2 Nephi 9–10 that has given you hope? What will you do to remember these things when you feel discouraged?

See also John 16:33.

Ideas for Family Scripture Study and Family Home Evening

As you read the scriptures with your family, the Spirit can help you know what principles to emphasize and discuss in order to meet the needs of your family. Here are some ideas.

2 Nephi 8:3–7. When you read 2 Nephi 8:3, you could show pictures of a desert and a garden. How does the Lord turn the deserts of our lives into gardens? In verses 4–7, what does the Lord counsel us to do in order to receive the joy described in verse 3?

2 Nephi 8:24–25. How can Isaiah's encouraging words to the people of Zion strengthen us in our efforts to become more faithful disciples of Jesus Christ? How is waking up and getting dressed similar to what God wants us to do spiritually?

2 Nephi 9:1–26. What could your family do to better understand the magnitude of Jesus Christ's "infinite atonement"? (verse 7). Perhaps they could look at or think about things that seem infinite in number—blades of grass in a field, grains of sand on a beach, or stars in the sky. How is the Savior's Atonement infinite? What phrases in 2 Nephi 9 deepen our gratitude for what the Savior did for us?

2 Nephi 9:27–44. Perhaps one day this week your family could search 2 Nephi 9:27–38, looking for the warnings (preceded by "wo"). Which of these seem especially important for your family to discuss? On another day, you could search 2 Nephi 9:39–44, looking for what Jacob invited his people to remember.

2 Nephi 9:28–29, 50–51. What are some examples of "the vainness, and the frailties, and the foolishness of men"? (verse 28). What can we do to place more value on the things of God and less on the things of the world?

2 Nephi 9:45. Your family might enjoy making a paper chain and then taking turns putting it on and shaking it off. How are sins like chains? How does the Savior help us shake them off?

For more ideas for teaching children, see this week's outline in *Come, Follow Me—For Primary*.

Improving Our Teaching

Be available and accessible. "Some of the best teaching moments start as a question or concern in the heart of a [family] member. . . . Let them know through your words and actions that you are eager to hear them" (*Teaching in the Savior's Way*, 16).

The Savior will save all God's children "if they will hearken unto his voice" (2 Nephi 9:21). *He Healed Many of Diverse Diseases,* by J. Kirk Richards

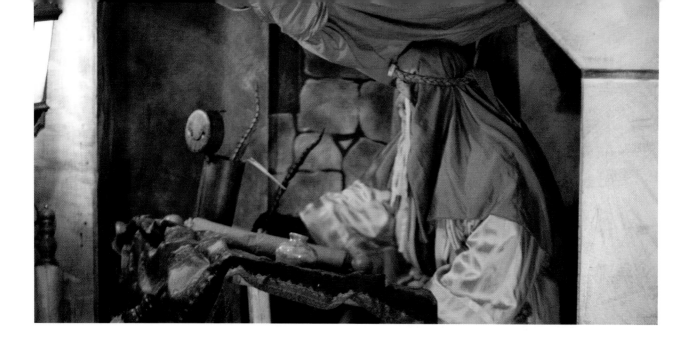

2 Nephi 11–25

"WE REJOICE IN CHRIST"

Nephi taught that Isaiah's words "are plain unto all those that are filled with the spirit of prophecy" (2 Nephi 25:4). As you read, seek the spirit of prophecy by preparing yourself spiritually, listening to the Spirit, and recording your impressions.

RECORD YOUR IMPRESSIONS_____

_____

_____

Engraving on metal plates is not easy, and space on Nephi's small plates was limited. So why would Nephi go to the tedious effort of copying a large amount of Isaiah's writings into his record? He did it "that whoso . . . shall see these words may lift up their hearts and rejoice" (2 Nephi 11:8). In a sense, the invitation to read Isaiah's writings is an invitation to rejoice. You can take delight, as Nephi did, in Isaiah's prophecies about the gathering of Israel, the coming of the Messiah, and the millennial peace promised to the righteous. You can rejoice that even in a day of "trouble, and darkness," you "have seen a great light" (2 Nephi 18:22; 19:2). You can rejoice that you can "draw water out of the wells of salvation" (2 Nephi 22:3). In other words, you can "rejoice in Christ" (2 Nephi 25:26).

Ideas for Personal Scripture Study

2 NEPHI 11–25

How can I better understand the teachings of Isaiah?

Nephi acknowledged that for some, "the words of Isaiah are not plain" (2 Nephi 25:4). This can certainly be true for those who aren't familiar with ancient Jewish culture and geography like Nephi was (see 2 Nephi 25:6). But Nephi also gave counsel to help us find meaning in Isaiah's writings:

"Liken his words unto" yourself (2 Nephi 11:2). Many of Isaiah's teachings have multiple possible meanings and applications. For example, his writings about the scattering and gathering of Israel might prompt you to think about your need to be "gathered" back to the Savior.

Seek to be "filled with the spirit of prophecy" (2 Nephi 25:4). The best way to understand Isaiah's prophecies is to seek inspiration from the Spirit. Pray for spiritual guidance. You may not understand everything all at once, but the Spirit can help you learn what you need to know for your life today.

You might also find it helpful to refer to the study helps in the scriptures, including the footnotes, chapter headings, Guide to the Scriptures, and so on.

2 NEPHI 11:2–8; 25:19–29

"The right way is to believe in Christ."

Nephi both introduced and concluded his quotation of Isaiah by expressing his testimony of Jesus Christ (see 2 Nephi 11:2–8; 25:19–29). What impresses you about his testimony? As you study this week, think about Nephi's desires to "persuade [his] children . . . to believe in Christ, and to be reconciled to God" (2 Nephi 25:23), and note passages that persuade *you* to believe in and follow Jesus Christ.

It might help to remember that many of Isaiah's teachings about the Savior are conveyed through symbols. For example, you may see the Savior in symbols such as the lord of a vineyard (see 2 Nephi 15:1–7), a stone (see 2 Nephi 18:14), and a light (see 2 Nephi 19:2). What other symbols of Jesus Christ do you find in these chapters? What do these symbols teach you about Him?

2 NEPHI 12–13

The proud and worldly will be humbled.

Nephi had foreseen that pride would cause the downfall of his people (see 1 Nephi 12:19). So it's not surprising that Nephi would share with his people Isaiah's repeated warnings against pride. In chapters 12 and 13, look for words that Isaiah used to describe pridefulness, such as *lofty* and *haughty*. Then you might try paraphrasing these warnings in your own words, as if you were writing a message to yourself to warn about pride.

See also "Chapter 18: Beware of Pride" (*Teachings of Presidents of the Church: Ezra Taft Benson* [2014], 229–40).

2 NEPHI 12:2–5; 21:9–12; 22; 24:1–3

In the Millennium, God's people will enjoy peace.

You might find it helpful to visualize yourself in the place of Nephi and his people. Imagine you fled from Jerusalem just before it was destroyed (see 2 Nephi 25:10), and now you are part of the scattering of Israel. How might it have felt to read Isaiah's teachings about the future gathering of Israel and a peaceful Millennium? As Latter-day Saints, we have been called to help gather God's people in the latter days in preparation for Christ's millennial reign. As you read these verses, ponder how you are helping fulfill the prophecies they describe. What do you feel inspired to do to help gather God's people?

Ideas for Family Scripture Study and Family Home Evening

As you read the scriptures with your family, the Spirit can help you know what principles to emphasize and discuss in order to meet the needs of your family. Here are some ideas.

2 Nephi 12:1–3. If you have been to the temple—"the mountain of the Lord's house"—you might share with your family how temple covenants are helping you "walk in [the Lord's] paths." If you have not been to the temple, reading these verses together might inspire a discussion about how you can prepare for temple blessings.

2 Nephi 15:18–23. Can your family think of modern examples of the unrighteous ideas that these verses describe? How can we avoid being deceived by false ideas about good and evil?

2 Nephi 21. If your family needs help understanding this chapter (which corresponds to Isaiah 11),

you might find insights in Doctrine and Covenants 113:1–6, in which the Prophet Joseph Smith answers some questions about Isaiah 11. What do we learn about Jesus Christ from these verses?

2 Nephi 21:9. What are some specific things we can do to help fill the earth with "the knowledge of the Lord"?

2 Nephi 25:23–26. How can you help your family members "rejoice in Christ"? Maybe you could invite them to write on slips of paper things about the Savior that bring them joy. Then, during future family home evenings or family scripture study, someone could read a slip. Family members could add slips throughout the year.

For more ideas for teaching children, see this week's outline in *Come, Follow Me—For Primary.*

Improving Personal Study

Look for patterns. In the scriptures we can find patterns that show us how the Lord works. For example, in 2 Nephi 11–25, you might find patterns that show how the Lord warns and forgives.

Panama City Panama Temple. "The Lord's house shall be established in the top of the mountains, . . . and all nations shall flow unto it" (2 Nephi 12:2).

He Will Lead Thee by the Hand, by Sandra Rast

2 Nephi 26–30

"A MARVELOUS WORK AND A WONDER"

The Lord said, "I command all . . . that they shall write the words which I speak unto them" (2 Nephi 29:11). Through the Spirit, the Lord will speak to you as you study His word. Record what you receive.

RECORD YOUR IMPRESSIONS_____

_____

_____

"I prophesy unto you concerning the last days," Nephi wrote (2 Nephi 26:14). In other words, he was writing about our day. And there's reason to be concerned about what he saw: people denying the power and miracles of God, rampant envy and strife, the devil binding people with strong cords. But in addition to these latter-day "works of darkness" (2 Nephi 26:10, 22) led by the adversary, Nephi also spoke of "a marvelous work and a wonder" led by the Lord Himself (2 Nephi 27:26). And at the center of that work would be a book—a book that speaks from the dust, that exposes Satan's lies, and that gathers the righteous like a standard. That book is the Book of Mormon, the marvelous work is the

work of the Lord's Church in the latter days, and the wonder is that He invites all of us, in spite of our weaknesses, to participate.

Ideas for Personal Scripture Study

2 NEPHI 26:20–33

Jesus Christ invites all to come unto Him.

The Prophet Joseph Smith taught that Heavenly Father is more "boundless in his mercies and blessings, than we are ready to believe or receive" (*The Joseph Smith Papers,* "History, 1838–1856, volume D-1," p. 4 [addenda], josephsmithpapers.org). Read what Nephi foresaw in 2 Nephi 26:20–22 and what he taught about the Savior in verses 23–33, and compare this to Joseph Smith's statement. What do you learn about the Lord's boundless mercy? What can you do as a member of Jesus Christ's Church to be more Christlike in the way you treat God's children?

See also 3 Nephi 18:30–32.

2 NEPHI 26–27
What is the book mentioned in these chapters?

Nephi's prophecy in 2 Nephi 26–27, which draws heavily from an earlier prophecy of Isaiah (see Isaiah 29), foretells the coming forth of the Book of Mormon. This prophecy describes the following:

- The words of Lehi's seed (his descendants) speaking from "low out of the dust" with a "familiar spirit" and being "sealed up in a book" (2 Nephi 26:14–17; see also Isaiah 29:4).

- A portion of the book being given to a learned man who says, "I cannot read it" (2 Nephi 27:15–20; Joseph Smith—History 1:64–65; see also Isaiah 29:11).

In addition to Isaiah, other biblical prophets allude to the Book of Mormon, although they don't mention it by name. For example, Ezekiel 37:15–20 speaks of a "stick of Joseph," which could refer to the record of the Nephites, who were descendants of Joseph. This record would become one with the "stick of Judah," meaning the Bible.

Other examples can be found in "Book of Mormon" (Guide to the Scriptures, scriptures.ChurchofJesusChrist.org).

2 NEPHI 28
Satan seeks to deceive.

Many of Satan's lies and tactics are exposed in Nephi's descriptions of the last days in 2 Nephi 28. See if you can find them (for example, see verses 6, 8, 21–23, 29). Why do you need to know about Satan's lies? What will you do when the adversary tries to deceive you?

2 NEPHI 28:27–31; 29
God continues to give revelation to guide His children.

As Latter-day Saints we are blessed with an abundance of the word of God, so Nephi's warnings can apply to us: we must never feel that "we have enough!" As you read the warnings in 2 Nephi 28 and 29, ponder questions like these:

- How does the Lord want me to feel about and respond to His word?

- Why are people sometimes "angry" about receiving more truth from God? (2 Nephi 28:28). Do I ever feel this way? If so, how can I become more receptive to truth?

- What does it mean to receive God's word? How can I show Him that I want to receive more of His word?

See also Alma 12:10–11; 3 Nephi 26:6–10.

2 NEPHI 29–30
God prepared the Book of Mormon for our day.

Nephi knew by revelation, even before the Book of Mormon had been completely written, that it would one day "be of great worth unto the children of men" (2 Nephi 28:2). Why is the Book of Mormon of great worth to you? Think about this question as you read 2 Nephi 29–30. What are some of the "marvelous" works that God is accomplishing in the world and in your life through the Book of Mormon?

Ideas for Family Scripture Study and Family Home Evening

As you read the scriptures with your family, the Spirit can help you know what principles to emphasize and discuss in order to meet the needs of your family. Here are some ideas.

2 Nephi 26:12–13. Nephi taught that Jesus Christ manifests Himself through the Holy Ghost. What experiences could family members share with each other when their testimonies of the Savior were strengthened by the Holy Ghost?

Nephi compared the devil's temptations to "a flaxen cord."

2 Nephi 26:22; 28:19–22. Maybe your family would enjoy an object lesson illustrating what 2 Nephi

26:22 teaches about the devil. As you read about Satan's tactics in 2 Nephi 28:19–22, you could wrap some thread around someone's wrists to represent "a flaxen cord." How is a flaxen cord like Satan's temptations? How might it become a strong cord? How can we detect Satan's lies?

2 Nephi 27:20–21. What might the Lord mean when He says, "I am able to do mine own work"? How does this truth influence the way we serve in His Church?

2 Nephi 28:30–31. Can your family think of something that, like revelation from God, is best received a little at a time? Why does God reveal truth to us "line upon line, precept upon precept, here a little and there a little" instead of all at once?

2 Nephi 29:7–9. What does the Lord intend to prove or show with the Book of Mormon?

For more ideas for teaching children, see this week's outline in *Come, Follow Me—For Primary.*

Improving Personal Study

Share insights. Discussing with others what you learn can strengthen your own understanding. After reading 2 Nephi 29:6–14, you may feel inspired to explain to a friend why we need the Book of Mormon.

Nephi's writings foretold "a marvelous work and a wonder" that would take place in the last days (2 Nephi 27:26).

Christ Teaching His Disciples, by Justin Kunz

2 Nephi 31–33

"THIS IS THE WAY"

This outline suggests principles you may find meaningful in 2 Nephi 31–33. But the most important things you'll learn in your study will come from the whisperings of the Spirit. Seek this guidance, and record the promptings that come.

RECORD YOUR IMPRESSIONS

Among Nephi's last recorded words, we find this declaration: "The Lord commanded me, and I must obey" (2 Nephi 33:15). This seems like a fitting summary of Nephi's life. He sought the will of the Lord and courageously strived to obey it—whether that meant risking his life to get the brass plates from Laban, building a boat and crossing the sea, or faithfully teaching the doctrine of Christ with plainness and power. Nephi could speak persuasively of the need to "press forward with a steadfastness in Christ," of following the "strait and narrow path which leads to eternal life" (2 Nephi 31:20, 18), because that is the path he followed. He knew by experience that this path, though demanding at times, is also joyful, and that "there is none other way nor name given under heaven whereby man can be saved in the kingdom of God" (2 Nephi 31:21).

Ideas for Personal Scripture Study

2 NEPHI 31–32

Jesus Christ and His doctrine are the only way to eternal life.

If you had to summarize the path to eternal life in just a few words, what would you say? Nephi, with his characteristic plainness and simplicity, did it this way: faith in Christ, repentance, baptism, receiving the gift of the Holy Ghost, and enduring to the end. After you study Nephi's teachings in 2 Nephi 31–32, consider how you would explain them to someone in your own words. Think about how living these teachings has blessed you. You might consider Nephi's teachings in 2 Nephi 31:18–20 and evaluate your own efforts to "press forward" along the gospel path.

See also 3 Nephi 11:32–39; 27:13–22; D. Todd Christofferson, "The Doctrine of Christ," *Ensign* or *Liahona,* May 2012, 86–90; Brian K. Ashton, "The Doctrine of Christ," *Ensign* or *Liahona,* Nov. 2016, 106–9.

Following Jesus Christ's teachings leads us to eternal life.

2 NEPHI 31:4–13

Jesus Christ set the perfect example of obedience when He was baptized.

Whether your baptism happened yesterday or 80 years ago, it was a pivotal moment—you entered a lifelong covenant to follow Jesus Christ. Think about your baptism as you read about the Savior's baptism in 2 Nephi 31:4–13. Why was the Savior baptized? How are the reasons He was baptized similar to the reasons you were baptized? What are you doing today to continue following the Savior's example of obedience?

The ordinance of the sacrament is a weekly opportunity for you to recommit to following Jesus Christ. The next time you partake of the sacrament, consider reading 2 Nephi 31:13 and pondering your determination to "follow the Son, with full purpose of heart" and your willingness "to take upon you the name of Christ."

2 NEPHI 31:17–20; 32

The Holy Ghost will show me what I should do.

If baptism and confirmation are "the gate by which [we] enter" the strait and narrow path (2 Nephi 31:17), what do we do once we're on the path? That's what Nephi's people wondered (see 2 Nephi 32:1). What answers did Nephi give in 2 Nephi 31:19–20 and chapter 32? What answers do you find for yourself?

See also David A. Bednar, "Receive the Holy Ghost," *Ensign* or *Liahona,* Nov. 2010, 94–97; "Holy Ghost," Gospel Topics, topics.ChurchofJesusChrist.org.

2 NEPHI 33

The Book of Mormon persuades all to believe in Christ.

In 2 Nephi 33, as Nephi concluded his writings, he explained reasons why he was writing in the first place. What reasons do you find in this chapter? Reflect on what you've read so far in 1 Nephi and 2 Nephi and notes you may have taken. How have the stories and teachings accomplished Nephi's purposes for you? For example, how have they persuaded you to "believe in [Christ], and to endure to the end"? (verse 4). Consider recording these experiences or sharing them with a family member or friend.

Ideas for Family Scripture Study and Family Home Evening

As you read the scriptures with your family, the Spirit can help you know what principles to emphasize and discuss in order to meet the needs of your family. Here are some ideas.

2 Nephi 31:5–13. Are any family members preparing for baptism, or have any been recently baptized? Perhaps they could share why they decided to get baptized. According to Nephi's teachings, what are some reasons we should be baptized? What are some blessings we receive when we are baptized?

2 Nephi 31:17–21. How can you help your family understand Nephi's analogy about the "strait and narrow path"? (2 Nephi 31:18). For instance, you could work together to draw a picture of the path that Nephi described in 2 Nephi 31:17–21, labeling it with the things we must do to enter the path and continue forward on it. How does the Savior help us progress along the path?

2 Nephi 31:20. If you want to help your family better understand how we endure to the end, page 6 of *Preach My Gospel* has a helpful definition; so does Elder Dale G. Renlund's message "Latter-day Saints Keep on Trying" (*Ensign* or *Liahona,* May 2015, 56–58).

2 Nephi 32:8–9. To help family members understand that we can "pray always," you could make a list of circumstances in which we could pray (or draw pictures to represent them). Then your family could sing a song that teaches about prayer, such as "Did You Think to Pray?" (*Hymns,* no. 140), replacing some of the words in the song with the words from their lists. How does the Lord bless us when we pray always?

2 Nephi 33:1–2. What might lead people to "harden their hearts against the Holy Spirit"? How can we make sure the Holy Ghost has "place in [us]"?

For more ideas for teaching children, see this week's outline in *Come, Follow Me—For Primary.*

Improving Our Teaching

Emulate the Savior. It is helpful to study how the Savior taught—the methods He used and the things He said. But Jesus's power to teach and lift others ultimately came from who He was and how He lived. The more diligently you strive to live like Jesus Christ and rely on His atoning power, the more naturally you will teach in His way.

To Fulfill All Righteousness, by Liz Lemon Swindle

Forgiven, by Greg K. Olsen

Jacob 1–4

BE RECONCILED UNTO GOD THROUGH THE ATONEMENT OF CHRIST

When you record spiritual impressions, you show that you want the Holy Ghost to teach you. As you read Jacob 1–4, consider writing down your insights.

RECORD YOUR IMPRESSIONS

The Nephites considered Nephi their "great protector" (Jacob 1:10). He had defended them against attacks from their enemies, and he had warned them about spiritual dangers. Now he was gone, and the task of leading the Nephites spiritually fell to Jacob, whom Nephi had consecrated to be a priest and teacher of the people (see Jacob 1:18). By inspiration, Jacob perceived that his people needed to be taught with "much boldness," for they were "beginning to labor in sin" (Jacob 2:7, 5). These sins were much like what people struggle with today: love of riches and sexual immorality. And yet while Jacob felt that he had to condemn this wickedness, his heart also ached for its victims, whose hearts had been "pierced with deep wounds" (Jacob 2:35). Jacob testified that healing for both groups—the sinner and the spiritually wounded—comes from the Savior Jesus Christ. Jacob's message, like the message of Nephi before him, was a call to "be reconciled unto [God] through the atonement of Christ" (Jacob 4:11).

Ideas for Personal Scripture Study

JACOB 1:6–8, 15–19; 2:1–11

The Lord wants me to magnify my calling.

To Jacob, teaching the word of God was more than an assignment from his brother—it was an "errand from the Lord," so he labored diligently to "magnify [his] office" (Jacob 1:17, 19). President Gordon B. Hinckley taught that we magnify our callings "as we serve with diligence, as we teach with faith and testimony, as we lift and strengthen and build convictions of righteousness in those whose lives we touch" ("Magnify Your Calling," *Ensign,* May 1989, 47). Think about your own "[errands] from the Lord" as you read Jacob 1:6–8, 15–19 and 2:1–11. Why did Jacob serve so faithfully? What does his example inspire you to do to magnify your Church callings and your responsibilities at home?

See also "Rise to Your Call" (video, ChurchofJesusChrist.org).

JACOB 2:23–3:12

The Lord delights in chastity.

Sin has consequences for individuals and for societies. In speaking about sexual sin, Jacob warned of both types of consequences. When you read Jacob 2:31–35 and 3:10, look for ways immorality was affecting the Nephites as a people and as individuals. How are these ways similar to the consequences of immorality you see in today's world? What do you find in Jacob's words that could help you teach a loved one about the importance of chastity? How have you been blessed by your efforts to be chaste?

Note that Jacob also addressed the practice of having more than one wife. What do you find in Jacob 2:23–30 that helps you understand why the Lord has, in limited situations, commanded His people to practice plural marriage? How does He feel about those who do so without His authorization?

JACOB 4

I can be reconciled to God through the Atonement of Jesus Christ.

Jacob pleaded with his people to "be reconciled unto [God] through the atonement of Christ" (Jacob 4:11). What do you think that means? Would it help to look up *reconcile* in a dictionary? Perhaps you can find words or phrases in this chapter that suggest to you how you can come unto Christ so that you can be reconciled to God. For example, Jacob taught that the law of Moses was given to point the people to Jesus Christ (see Jacob 4:5). What has God provided to point you to Christ? How are you using these things to draw closer to God?

See also 2 Nephi 10:24.

JACOB 4:8–18

I can avoid spiritual blindness by focusing on the Savior.

As Jacob sought to turn his people more completely to the Lord, he warned them not to be spiritually blind and not to despise the gospel's "words of plainness" (see Jacob 4:13–14). Elder Quentin L. Cook warned of similar problems in our day: "There is a tendency among some of us to 'look beyond the mark' rather than to maintain a testimony of gospel basics. We do this when we substitute the philosophies of men for gospel truths, engage in gospel extremism, . . . or elevate rules over doctrine. Avoiding these behaviors will help us avoid the theological blindness and stumbling that Jacob described" ("Looking beyond the Mark," *Ensign,* Mar. 2003, 42).

According to Jacob 4:8–18, what can we do to focus on the Savior and avoid spiritual blindness?

Ideas for Family Scripture Study and Family Home Evening

As you read the scriptures with your family, the Spirit can help you know what principles to emphasize and discuss in order to meet the needs of your family. Here are some ideas.

Jacob 1:6–8, 15–19; 2:1–11; 4:18. What words and phrases in these verses convey the love Jacob felt for those he led? What have our Church leaders done to help us feel their "desire and anxiety for the welfare of [our] souls"? (Jacob 2:3). Perhaps family members could share ways we can sustain our Church leaders. You could plan to do something as a family for local Church leaders, such as writing notes to thank them for their service or remembering them and their families in your prayers.

Jacob 2:8. How does the word of God heal "the wounded soul"?

Jacob 2:12–21. What do these verses teach about how we should view material wealth? What are we doing to reach out to others who need our help?

Jacob 3:1–2. What does it mean to be "pure in heart" and "look unto God with firmness of mind"?

Jacob 4:4–11. One way to help your family understand what it means to be "unshaken" in their faith would be to find a large tree nearby and ask family members to shake individual branches. Then let them try to shake the trunk. Why is it harder to shake the trunk? What can we learn from Jacob's teachings about how to develop faith that is "unshaken"?

Like the trunk of a tree, our faith in Christ can be "unshaken."

For more ideas for teaching children, see this week's outline in *Come, Follow Me—For Primary*.

Improving Personal Study

Listen to the Spirit. As you study, pay attention to your thoughts and feelings (see D&C 8:2–3), even if they seem unrelated to what you are reading. Those impressions may be the very things God wants you to know and do.

I Will Send Their Words Forth (Jacob the Teacher), by Elspeth Caitlin Young

Allegory of the Olive Tree, by Brad Teare

MARCH 16–22

Jacob 5–7

THE LORD LABORS WITH US

Reading the scriptures invites revelation. So as you read Jacob 5–7, seek guidance from the Spirit to help you and your family. What messages does the Lord have for you?

RECORD YOUR IMPRESSIONS

There are many, many people who haven't yet heard the gospel of Jesus Christ. If you ever feel overwhelmed by the immensity of the task of gathering them into the Lord's Church, the allegory of the olive trees in Jacob 5 has a reassuring reminder: the vineyard belongs to the Lord. He has given each of us a small area to assist in His work—our family, our circle of friends, our sphere of influence. And sometimes the first person we help gather is ourselves.

But we are never alone in this work, for the Lord of the vineyard labors alongside His servants (see Jacob 5:72). God knows and loves His children, and He will prepare a way for each of them to hear His gospel, even those who have rejected Him in the past (see Jacob 4:15–18). And then, when the work is done, all those who have been "diligent in laboring with [Him] . . . shall have joy with [Him] because of the fruit of [His] vineyard" (Jacob 5:75).

Ideas for Personal Scripture Study

JACOB 5–6

What is an allegory?

Allegories are stories that teach spiritual truths through symbols. In the allegory of the olive trees, for example, a vineyard represents the world, a tame olive tree represents Israel (those who have made covenants with God), and wild olive trees represent the gentile nations (those who have not made covenants with God).

As you study the allegory in Jacob 5, look for additional symbols and ponder what they might mean. For example, what do you think the good fruit represents? What could the bad fruit symbolize?

JACOB 5; 6:3–5

Jesus Christ is the Lord of the vineyard.

Before you begin your study of the allegory of the olive trees in Jacob 5, it might be helpful to review Jacob 4:10–18 to learn why Jacob felt inspired to share this allegory with his people. In Jacob 6:3–5, you can find some additional messages that Jacob wanted to emphasize; look for these messages in the allegory. What messages do you find for yourself in Jacob 5?

Jacob 5 is a long chapter—the longest in the Book of Mormon. Perhaps it would help to divide it into the following sections, which describe periods of the world's history:

Verses 3–14. The scattering of Israel before the time of Christ

Verses 15–28. The ministry of Christ and the Apostles

Verses 29–49. The Great Apostasy

Verses 50–76. The gathering of Israel in the latter days

Verses 76–77. The Millennium and end of the world

For additional insights about the allegory, see the diagram that accompanies this outline.

We can all serve God by helping Him gather His children.

JACOB 5:61–75

God invites me to help Him gather His children.

The "other servants" (Jacob 5:70) who were called into the Lord's vineyard include people like you—as members of the Church, we are all responsible to help God gather His children. What principles do you find in Jacob 5, especially verses 61–62 and 70–75, about working in the Lord's vineyard? How have you felt Him call you to serve in His vineyard? What experiences have you had while participating in His work?

See also "Missionary Work," Gospel Topics, topics.ChurchofJesusChrist.org; "Old Testament Olive Vineyard," "Help the Church Grow" (videos, ChurchofJesusChrist.org).

JACOB 7:1–23

I can stand strong when others challenge my faith.

The Nephites' experience with Sherem is often repeated today: there may be learned, well-spoken people who try to destroy your faith. But Jacob "could not be shaken" (Jacob 7:5). How did Jacob respond when his faith was attacked? What do you learn from his responses? What can you do now to prepare for times when your faith will be challenged?

See also "Answering Gospel Questions," Gospel Topics, topics.ChurchofJesusChrist.org; Jeffrey R. Holland, "The Cost—and Blessings—of Discipleship," *Ensign* or *Liahona,* May 2014, 6–9.

Ideas for Family Scripture Study and Family Home Evening

As you read the scriptures with your family, the Spirit can help you know what principles to emphasize and discuss in order to meet the needs of your family. Here are some ideas.

Jacob 5. Some families have found it helpful to draw the symbols from the allegory of the olive trees as they read it. Your family might enjoy that approach, or there could be another way you can help family members visualize the symbols in the allegory. Maybe you could mark an area on a table or floor to represent the vineyard (or the world) and depict the tame olive tree (or the house of Israel) with an object, such as a puzzle, that can be divided into pieces (to represent the scattering of Israel) and then brought back together (to represent the gathering of Israel). What does this allegory teach us about the Lord? about His servants?

Jacob 5:70–77. As you read about the "last time" that the Lord labors in His vineyard, what inspires you and your family to serve the Lord "with your might"? (Jacob 5:71). You could invite family members to personalize verse 75 by adding their names into this verse—for example, "Blessed art thou [name]." Maybe they can share experiences in which they felt joy while serving the Lord of the vineyard, for example through sharing the gospel, serving in the temple, or strengthening Church members. (See also M. Russell Ballard, "Put Your Trust in the Lord," *Ensign* or *Liahona,* Nov. 2013, 43–45.)

Jacob 6:4–7. How has the Lord extended His arm of mercy toward us? What does the word "cleave" mean in these verses? How does the Lord cleave unto us? How can we cleave unto Him?

Jacob 7:1–12. What do we learn from these verses about how people try to lead others astray? How can we follow Jacob's example and be steadfast in our faith in Christ?

For more ideas for teaching children, see this week's outline in *Come, Follow Me—For Primary.*

Improving Our Teaching

Memorize a scripture. Select a scripture passage that is particularly meaningful to your family, and memorize it together. Elder Richard G. Scott taught, "A memorized scripture becomes an enduring friend that is not weakened with the passage of time" ("The Power of Scripture," *Ensign* or *Liahona,* Nov. 2011, 6).

The Allegory of the Olive Trees (Jacob 5)

First Visit	Second Visit	Third Visit	Fourth Visit	The Millennium
Before the Time of Christ (verses 3–14)	The Time of Christ (verses 15–28)	The Great Apostasy (verses 29–49)	The Restoration of the Gospel (verses 50–76)	(verses 76–77)
God sees the apostasy of ancient Israel. He sends prophets to cry repentance, but few people listen. He allows the wicked to be destroyed and brings in the Gentiles. A few righteous branches of Israel are scattered around the world.	As Christ's Church spreads, Israel and most of the scattered branches produce good fruit.	All the fruit becomes corrupt, including the natural branches that were scattered.	Scattered Israel is gathered, and the gospel is taken to all the world. As righteousness increases, the wicked are destroyed until no wickedness remains (the Second Coming of Jesus Christ).	Righteousness prevails. When evil again enters the world, God will separate the righteous from the wicked and cleanse the earth by fire.

All trees become as one and bear natural fruit (verses 74–76)

Good fruit will be gathered out and the vineyard will be burned (verse 77)

Branches of the scattered trees are grafted back into original tree (verses 52–53)

Wild branches are burned (verses 58, 65–66)

Branches of the original tree are grafted into the scattered trees (verses 54–56)

Evil fruit, but the roots are still good (verses 29–37)

Evil fruit (verses 39, 46)

Evil fruit (verses 39, 46)

Evil fruit (verses 39, 46)

Evil fruit (verses 39, 46)

Good fruit (verses 15–18)

Poor ground, good fruit (verses 20–22)

Poorer ground, good fruit (verse 23)

Fruit (verse 24; branch not mentioned again)

Good ground, good and bad fruit (verse 25)

Tame olive tree (Israel) is dying (verses 3–4). The master prunes and fertilizes; a few new branches grow, but the top is still dying (verses 4–6)

Main branches are removed, and wild branches are grafted in; tender branches are hidden (verses 7–14)

Withered branches are burned (verses 7, 9)

Wild olive tree (Gentiles; verses 7, 9)

Jacob and Enos, by Scott Snow

Enos–Words of Mormon

HE WORKS IN ME TO DO HIS WILL

As you read Enos through Words of Mormon, look for messages that will be valuable to you or your family.

RECORD YOUR IMPRESSIONS

Enos went to the forest to hunt beasts, but he ended up staying there to pray "all the day long . . . and when the night came" (Enos 1:3–4). Because his soul was truly hungry to receive a remission of his sins, Enos was willing to pray as long as necessary and even to "wrestle" before God (Enos 1:2). That's what sincere prayer is: not so much asking for anything we want but a sincere effort to commune with God and align our will to His. When you pray in this way, when your voice has "reached the heavens," you discover as Enos did that God hears you, and He truly cares about you, your loved ones, and even your enemies (see Enos 1:4–17). In those moments, God can make His will known to you, and you'll be more willing and able to do His will because you are in harmony with Him. Like Mormon, you may "not know all things; but the Lord knoweth all things . . . [and] he worketh in [you] to do according to his will" (Words of Mormon 1:7).

Ideas for Personal Scripture Study

A parent's words can have a lasting influence.

What messages do these verses have for parents and for children?

My heartfelt prayers will be answered.

Enos's experience with prayer is one of the most memorable in scripture. Your experiences may be less dramatic, but they don't have to be less meaningful. Enos's experiences might reveal ways to improve your prayers. Here are some questions to ponder:

- What words describe Enos's efforts as he prayed?

- What did Enos initially pray for? (see Enos 1:4). What can you learn from Enos's response after he received an answer? (see Enos 1:5–7).

- How did Enos act on the answers he received?

- What can you learn from Enos about how to have "unshaken" faith in the Lord? (Enos 1:11).

The Lord will bless me when I keep the commandments.

One of God's most repeated promises in the Book of Mormon is that if the Nephites kept the commandments, they would prosper (see 2 Nephi 1:20; Jarom 1:9–12; Omni 1:6). The books of Jarom and Omni show a few ways in which this promise was fulfilled. What do you learn from these accounts that can help you "prosper in the land"?

Who were the people of Zarahemla?

After the Nephites fled the land of Nephi, they discovered a numerous people living in a place called Zarahemla. The people of Zarahemla were descendants of a group of Israelites who, like Lehi's family, had left Jerusalem and were led by God to the promised land. Among that group was Mulek, one of the sons of Zedekiah, the king of Judah who was captured by the Babylonians in about 587 BC (see Jeremiah 52:1–11; Mosiah 25:2; Helaman 8:21).

After the people of Zarahemla arrived in the promised land, they met Coriantumr (see Omni 1:21), the last known survivor of the Jaredites, whose story is told in the book of Ether.

What is Words of Mormon?

Words of Mormon serves as a bridge between the two sets of plates that make up the Book of Mormon. Here Mormon gives an explanation of these two records, and his words teach an important message about trusting the Lord, even when we don't fully understand His direction.

As Nephi was writing the record of his people, God directed him to create two sets of plates, called the small plates and the large plates of Nephi. Nephi didn't know why he was commanded to create two sets of plates, but he trusted that the Lord had "a wise purpose . . . , which purpose I know not" (1 Nephi 9:5; see also "A Brief Explanation about the Book of Mormon").

Centuries later, as Mormon was abridging Nephi's large plates, he came across the small plates. The small plates covered many of the same events described in the large plates that Mormon had already abridged, but the small plates focused more on spiritual matters and the ministry and teachings of the prophets. God inspired Mormon to include the small plates of Nephi in his record in addition to the large plates.

Like Nephi, Mormon didn't understand God's purpose for having both sets of plates, but he trusted that it was "for a wise purpose" (Words of Mormon 1:7).

Today we know what God's purpose was. In 1828, after Joseph Smith had translated part of Mormon's abridgment of Nephi's large plates (116 manuscript pages), Martin Harris lost those pages. God commanded Joseph not to retranslate this portion because evil men would change the words and try to discredit Joseph (see D&C 10, section heading; D&C 10:14–19, 30–45). Thankfully, God had foreseen this and provided the small plates, which covered the same history that was lost with the 116 pages. The small plates compose the books that come before Words of Mormon, and Mormon's abridgment of the large plates begins after the Words of Mormon.

Mormon Compiling the Plates, by Jorge Cocco

Ideas for Family Scripture Study and Family Home Evening

As you read the scriptures with your family, the Spirit can help you know what principles to emphasize and discuss in order to meet the needs of your family. Here are some ideas.

Enos 1:1–17. Your family could look at a picture of Enos praying and search Enos 1:1–17 for phrases that could be used as a title for the picture. You could also ask family members to draw pictures of Enos's experience. What do we learn from Enos about seeking forgiveness?

Jarom 1:2. How has our study of the Book of Mormon "revealed the plan of salvation" to us?

Omni 1:12–22. What do these verses teach about the importance of having the word of God in our lives?

Words of Mormon 1:3–9. How will we be blessed by keeping personal and family records? How can we make our records more focused on Christ?

For more ideas for teaching children, see this week's outline in *Come, Follow Me—For Primary*.

Improving Our Teaching

Gather together often. President Henry B. Eyring taught: "Never miss a chance to gather children together to learn of the doctrine of Jesus Christ. Such moments are so rare in comparison with the efforts of the enemy" ("The Power of Teaching Doctrine," *Ensign*, May 1999, 74).

Enos Praying, by Robert T. Barrett

Christ and the Apostles, by Del Parson

Easter

"HE SHALL RISE . . . WITH HEALING IN HIS WINGS"

During the days leading up to Easter Sunday, consider focusing your personal and family scripture study on the Book of Mormon's powerful testimony of the life, death, Resurrection, and atoning power of Jesus Christ.

RECORD YOUR IMPRESSIONS_____

_____

_____

The ancient Apostles were bold in their testimonies of Jesus Christ and His Resurrection. Millions believe in Jesus Christ and strive to follow Him because of their words recorded in the Bible. Yet some might wonder, if Jesus Christ is the Savior of the whole world, then why were His eyewitnesses limited to a handful of people concentrated in one small region?

The Book of Mormon stands as an additional, convincing witness that Jesus Christ *is* the Savior of the world, "manifesting himself unto all nations" (title page of the Book of Mormon) and offering salvation to all who come unto Him. In addition, this second witness also clarifies what salvation means. This is why Nephi, Jacob, Mormon, and all the prophets labored so "diligently to engraven these words upon plates"—to declare to future generations that they too "knew of Christ, and . . . had a hope of his glory" (Jacob 4:3–4). This Easter season, reflect on the testimonies in the Book of Mormon that the power of Christ's Atonement is both universal and personal—redeeming the whole world and redeeming you.

Ideas for Personal Scripture Study

2 NEPHI 9:6–15, 22; ALMA 11:41–45; 40:21–23; 3 NEPHI 26:4–5

Because of Jesus Christ's Resurrection, all people will be resurrected.

It's traditional at Easter to ponder the Resurrection of Jesus Christ, but what exactly does it mean to be resurrected? What insights does the Book of Mormon offer about resurrection? Perhaps as part of your Easter observance you could list truths about resurrection that you find in 2 Nephi 9:6–15, 22; Alma 11:41–45; 40:21–23; and 3 Nephi 26:4–5. You could also record why you think it's important to know each of these truths.

You might notice that truths about the Resurrection are often taught in conjunction with truths about the Final Judgment. Ponder what that teaches you about the importance of the Resurrection in the plan of salvation.

See also Luke 24:36–43; Acts 24:15; 1 Corinthians 15:12–23.

Gethsemane, by Michael T. Malm

MOSIAH 3:7; 15:5–9; ALMA 7:11–13

Jesus Christ took upon Himself my sins, pains, and infirmities.

The Bible clearly teaches that Jesus Christ atoned for our sins. The Book of Mormon, however, expands our understanding of Christ's sacrifice and suffering in important ways. You can find some of these teachings in Mosiah 3:7; 15:5–9; and Alma 7:11–13. After you read these passages, consider recording what you discover in a chart like this one:

What did the Savior suffer?	Why did He suffer?	What does this mean to me?

See also Isaiah 53; Hebrews 4:14–16.

MOSIAH 5:1–2; 27:8–28; ALMA 15:3–12; 24:7–19

The Atonement of Jesus Christ cleanses me and helps perfect me.

It could be said that the Book of Mormon is largely an account of people who changed because of the Atonement of Jesus Christ. In fact, some of those people committed grievous sins and were even enemies of God's people before the Savior's power worked in them a mighty change according to their faith in Him. You can read some of these experiences in Mosiah 5:1–2; 27:8–28; and Alma 15:3–12; 24:7–19; you might think of other examples to study as well. What do you notice that each of these experiences has in common? What differences do you notice? What do these accounts teach you about how the Savior's Atonement can change you?

See also Alma 5:6–14; 13:11–12; 18; 19:1–16; 22:1–26; 36:16–21; Ether 12:27; Moroni 10:32–33.

Ideas for Family Scripture Study and Family Home Evening

As you celebrate Easter with your family, look for ways to learn together about the Savior and His Atonement, including the Resurrection. Here are some ideas.

3 Nephi 11; 17. Some families have found that studying the account of the resurrected Savior's visit to the Americas is especially meaningful during the Easter season. Encourage family members to imagine what it would have been like to feel His wounds (see 3 Nephi 11:14–15) or to be one of the children He blessed (see 3 Nephi 17:21). How does this account deepen our gratitude for the Savior's Resurrection? A painting that depicts this account accompanies this outline; others can be found at ChurchofJesusChrist.org. Your family members might also enjoy drawing their own pictures of what they read.

Messages from general conference. In many parts of the world, this year's April general conference takes place the weekend before Easter. Perhaps listening to the conference messages could help your family focus on the Savior this Easter. For example, you could invite family members to listen for conference messages that testify of Jesus Christ and His Resurrection—especially from the Apostles, who are special witnesses of Jesus Christ. Then you could review these messages together and identify teachings that strengthen your testimonies of the Savior.

"The Living Christ: The Testimony of the Apostles." As a family, read "The Living Christ: The Testimony of the Apostles" (*Ensign* or *Liahona,* May 2017, inside front cover; see also ChurchofJesusChrist.org) and invite each family member to pick an Easter message from this testimony to share with others. For example, you might create posters to display on social media, on your front door, or in a window.

Videos: Special Witnesses of Christ. ChurchofJesusChrist.org and the Gospel Library app have a video series called *Special Witnesses of Christ.* It includes videos of each member of the First Presidency and Quorum of the Twelve Apostles bearing testimony of Jesus Christ. Your family could watch one or more of these videos and discuss what they teach us about what the Savior has done for us.

For more ideas for teaching children, see this week's outline in *Come, Follow Me—For Primary.*

Improving Our Teaching

Live the gospel of Jesus Christ. The most important thing you can do as a parent is to live the gospel with all your heart. This is the best way to qualify for the companionship of the Holy Ghost. You don't have to be perfect, just diligently trying to do your best and seeking forgiveness through the Savior's Atonement. (See *Teaching in the Savior's Way,* 13–14.)

Illustration of Christ with the Nephites by Ben Sowards

Minerva K. Teichert (1888–1976), *King Benjamin's Farewell Address*, 1935, oil on masonite, 36 x 48 inches. Brigham Young University Museum of Art.

Mosiah 1–3

"FILLED WITH LOVE TOWARDS GOD AND ALL MEN"

King Benjamin gave one reason for recording our spiritual impressions: "It were not possible that our father, Lehi, could have remembered all these things, to have taught them to his children, except it were for the help of these plates" (Mosiah 1:4).

RECORD YOUR IMPRESSIONS_____

_____

_____

When you hear the word *king,* you might think of crowns, castles, servants, and thrones. In Mosiah 1–3, you will read about a different kind of king. Rather than living off the labors of his people, King Benjamin "labored with [his] own hands" (Mosiah 2:14). Instead of having others serve him, he served his people "with all the might, mind and strength which the Lord [had] granted unto [him]" (Mosiah 2:11). This king did not want his people to worship him; rather, he taught them to worship a King greater than himself, for he understood that it is "the Lord Omnipotent who reigneth" (Mosiah 3:5). Like all great leaders in the kingdom of God, King Benjamin's words and example point us to the Heavenly King, who is the Savior, Jesus Christ. King Benjamin testified that Jesus came "down from heaven" and went "forth amongst men, working mighty miracles. . . . And lo, he cometh unto his own, that salvation might come unto the children of men even through faith on his name" (Mosiah 3:5, 9).

Ideas for Personal Scripture Study

MOSIAH 2:1–9

Receiving the word of God requires preparation.

When King Benjamin sent word that he wanted to speak to his people, so many people came "that they did not number them" (Mosiah 2:2). They came, in part, because of their gratitude and love for their leader. But more important, they came to be taught the word of God.

As you read Mosiah 2:1–9, look for what the people did to show that they valued God's word. What did King Benjamin ask them to do to prepare to hear God's word? (see verse 9). How can you better prepare yourself to receive the word of God in your personal and family study and during Church meetings?

See also Matthew 13:18–23; Alma 16:16–17.

When I serve others, I am also serving God.

MOSIAH 2:10–26

When I serve others, I am also serving God.

Do you struggle to find time to serve or wish that your service brought you more joy? What do you think King Benjamin would say if you asked him why he served with all his "might, mind, and strength"? (Mosiah 2:11). As you read Mosiah 2:10–26, identify the truths that King Benjamin taught about service and ponder how you can use them in your life. For example, what does it mean to you to know that when you serve other people, you are also serving God? (see Mosiah 2:17). Think of a way you can serve someone this week!

See also Matthew 25:40.

MOSIAH 3:1–20

I can overcome the natural man and become a saint through the Atonement of Jesus Christ.

King Benjamin, like all prophets, testified of Jesus Christ so that his people "might receive remission of their sins, and rejoice with exceedingly great joy" (Mosiah 3:13). He also taught that the Savior, through His Atonement, not only makes us clean but also gives us power to put off the "natural man" and become "a saint" (Mosiah 3:19; see also Guide to the Scriptures, "Natural Man," scriptures.ChurchofJesusChrist.org).

Elder David A. Bednar explained: "It is the Atonement of Jesus Christ that provides both a *cleansing and redeeming power* that helps us to overcome sin and a *sanctifying and strengthening power* that helps us to become better than we ever could by relying only upon our own strength. The infinite Atonement is for both the sinner and for the saint in each of us" ("Clean Hands and a Pure Heart," *Ensign* or *Liahona,* Nov. 2007, 82).

Here are some questions to ponder as you read King Benjamin's testimony of the Savior in Mosiah 3:1–20:

- What do I learn from these verses about the Savior and His mission?

- How has Jesus Christ helped me overcome sin? How has He helped me change my nature and become more like a saint?

- What do I learn about becoming a saint from Mosiah 3:19?

MOSIAH 3:8

Why did King Benjamin refer to Jesus as "the Father of heaven and earth"?

President Joseph F. Smith explained: "Jesus Christ, whom we also know as Jehovah, was the executive of the Father, Elohim, in the work of creation. . . . Jesus Christ, being the Creator, is consistently called the Father of heaven and earth . . . ; and since His creations are of eternal quality He is very properly called the Eternal Father of heaven and earth" (*Teachings of Presidents of the Church: Joseph F. Smith* [1998], 357).

Ideas for Family Scripture Study and Family Home Evening

As you read the scriptures with your family, the Spirit can help you know what principles to emphasize and discuss in order to meet the needs of your family. Here are some ideas.

Mosiah 1:1–7. How did the plates of brass and the plates of Nephi bless King Benjamin's people? How do the scriptures bless our family?

Mosiah 2–3. It might be fun for your family to create the setting for King Benjamin's speech. You could make a small tower and let family members take turns reading King Benjamin's words while standing on it. The rest of the family could listen from inside a makeshift tent.

Mosiah 2:9–19. What do we learn about service from King Benjamin's teachings and example? What do we feel inspired to do?

Mosiah 2:15–25. Would it benefit your family to have a discussion about humility? Why did King Benjamin not boast about all he had done? What can we learn from his teachings about our relationship with God?

Mosiah 2:36–41. What did King Benjamin teach about the consequences of knowing truth but not living it? What did he teach about how to obtain true happiness?

Mosiah 3:19. What do we need to do to become saints? Which characteristic from this verse can we focus on developing as a family?

For more ideas for teaching children, see this week's outline in *Come, Follow Me—For Primary*.

Improving Personal Study

Set manageable goals. Spending even a few minutes a day studying the scriptures can bless your life. Commit to studying each day, and find a way to remind yourself of your commitment.

King Benjamin's Address, by Jeremy Winborg

In the Service of Your God, by Walter Rane

APRIL 20–26

Mosiah 4–6

"A MIGHTY CHANGE"

As you read and ponder Mosiah 4–6, pay attention to the promptings of the Holy Ghost. What good things are you inspired to do? (see Mosiah 5:2).

RECORD YOUR IMPRESSIONS

Have you ever heard someone speak and felt inspired to change your life? Perhaps you decided, because of what you heard, to live a little differently—or even a lot differently. King Benjamin's sermon was that kind of sermon, and the truths he taught had that kind of effect on the people who heard them. King Benjamin shared with his people what an angel had taught him—that wonderful blessings were possible through "the atoning blood of Christ" (Mosiah 4:2). His message changed their entire view of themselves (see Mosiah 4:2), changed their desires (see Mosiah 5:2), and inspired them to covenant with God that they would always do His will (see Mosiah 5:5). This is how King Benjamin's words affected his people. How will they affect you?

Ideas for Personal Scripture Study

MOSIAH 4

Through Jesus Christ, I can receive and retain a remission of my sins.

Overcoming the natural man isn't easy. It requires great effort to become "a saint through the atonement of Christ the Lord" (Mosiah 3:19). Sometimes, even when you have felt forgiven of your sins, you might struggle to keep that feeling and stay on the path of righteousness. King Benjamin taught his people how to both *receive* and *retain* a remission of sins and live consistently as a saint. As you study chapter 4 of Mosiah, you might ask yourself questions such as these:

Verses 1–12. What blessings did a remission of sins bring to King Benjamin's people? What did King Benjamin teach to help them retain the remission of their sins? What did he teach about how we receive salvation? Note what King Benjamin said we should "always retain in remembrance" (verse 11). What do you feel inspired to do to remember these things?

Verses 12–16. According to these verses, what happens in our lives if we do the things described in verse 11? Have you experienced these changes in your life? How do they relate to the changes described in Mosiah 3:19?

Verses 16–30. How does sharing with the poor help us retain a remission of our sins? How can you apply verse 27 to your efforts to be Christlike?

See also David A. Bednar, "Always Retain a Remission of Your Sins," *Ensign* or *Liahona,* May 2016, 59–62; Dale G. Renlund, "Preserving the Heart's Mighty Change," *Ensign* or *Liahona,* Nov. 2009, 97–99.

MOSIAH 5:1–7

The Spirit of the Lord can cause a mighty change in my heart.

It is not uncommon for people to say, "I can't change. That's just the way I am." In contrast, the experience of King Benjamin's people shows us how the Spirit of the Lord can truly change our hearts. President Russell M. Nelson taught: "We can change our behavior. Our very desires can change. . . . True change—permanent change—can come only through the healing, cleansing, and enabling power of the Atonement of Jesus Christ. . . . The gospel of Jesus Christ *is* a gospel of change!" ("Decisions for Eternity," *Ensign* or *Liahona,* Nov. 2013, 108).

The Savior can change our hearts and our lives. *Healing Hands,* by Adam Abram

As you read about the change that King Benjamin's people experienced, think about how the "mighty change" leading to true conversion has happened—or can happen—in your life. Have a few "mighty" moments led to your change of heart, or has your conversion happened more gradually?

See also Ezekiel 36:26–27; Alma 5:14; David A. Bednar, "Converted unto the Lord," *Ensign* or *Liahona,* Nov. 2012, 106–9.

MOSIAH 5:5–15

I take upon myself the name of Christ when I make covenants.

One reason King Benjamin wanted to address his people was to "give this people a name." Some were Nephites and others were descendants of Mulek, but these weren't the names he had in mind. He invited the people to take upon themselves "the name of Christ" as part of their covenant of obedience to God (Mosiah 1:11; 5:10). What do you learn from Mosiah 5:7–9 about what it means to take upon yourself the name of Christ?

Elder D. Todd Christofferson taught, "The source [of moral and spiritual power] is God. Our access to that power is through our covenants with Him" ("The Power of Covenants," *Ensign* or *Liahona,* May 2009, 20). As you read Mosiah 5:5–15, make a list of the blessings that will come into your life as you keep the covenants you have made with God. How does keeping your covenants help you retain the "mighty change" wrought in you through Jesus Christ and His Atonement?

Ideas for Family Scripture Study and Family Home Evening

As you read the scriptures with your family, the Spirit can help you know what principles to emphasize and discuss in order to meet the needs of your family. Here are some ideas.

Mosiah 4:9–12. How can your family more fully "believe in God" (Mosiah 4:9) and "always retain in remembrance, the greatness of God"? (Mosiah 4:11). Perhaps family members could read Mosiah 4:9–12 and identify phrases that help build their faith in God. Then they could write down these phrases and place them around the home as reminders. How will remembering these things help us "always rejoice" and "retain a remission of [our] sins"? (Mosiah 4:12).

Mosiah 4:14–15. What do we learn about fighting and quarrelling from these verses?

Mosiah 4:16–26. In what sense are we all beggars? According to these verses, how should we treat all of God's children? (see Mosiah 4:26). Who needs our help?

Mosiah 4:27. Is your family running faster than you have strength? Maybe you could invite family members to evaluate their activities to make sure they are being diligent but also wise.

Mosiah 5:5–15. What does taking the name of Christ upon us suggest about our relationship with Him? It might help to talk about why people sometimes write their names on their belongings. How can we show that we "belong" to the Savior?

For more ideas for teaching children, see this week's outline in *Come, Follow Me—For Primary.*

Improving Our Teaching

Nurture a loving atmosphere. The way family members treat each other can profoundly influence the spirit of your home. Help all family members do their part to establish a loving, respectful home so that everyone will feel safe sharing experiences, questions, and testimonies. (See *Teaching in the Savior's Way,* 15.)

In His Constant Care, by Greg K. Olsen

Minerva Teichert (1888-1976), *Ammon before King Limhi*, 1949-1951, oil on masonite, 35 15/16 x 48 inches. Brigham Young University Museum of Art, 1969.

Mosiah 7–10

"IN THE STRENGTH OF THE LORD"

As you read, the Spirit may bring to your attention certain phrases or passages. Write down how you feel that those passages apply to you.

RECORD YOUR IMPRESSIONS

While King Mosiah's people were enjoying "continual peace" in Zarahemla (Mosiah 7:1), their thoughts turned to another group of Nephites, who many years before had left to dwell in the land of Lehi-Nephi. Generations had passed, and Mosiah's people had heard nothing from them. So Mosiah asked Ammon to lead a search party to find the Nephites who had left. The search party found that the Nephites, "because of iniquity" (Mosiah 7:24), were in captivity to the Lamanites. But with the arrival of Ammon and his brethren, suddenly there was hope for deliverance.

Sometimes we're like these captive Nephites, suffering because of our sins, wondering how we'll ever find peace again. Sometimes we're like Ammon, feeling prompted to reach out to others and eventually finding that our efforts have inspired them to "lift up [their] heads, and rejoice, and put [their] trust in God" (Mosiah 7:19). No matter our circumstances, we all need to repent and "turn to the Lord with full purpose of heart," with faith that "he will . . . deliver [us]" (Mosiah 7:33).

Ideas for Personal Scripture Study

If I turn to the Lord, trust Him, and serve Him, He will deliver me.

Meeting Ammon, who was a Nephite from Zarahemla, gave King Limhi a spark of hope, and he wanted to pass that hope on to his people. As you read Mosiah 7:14–33, notice what Limhi said to his people to encourage them, strengthen their faith, and give them hope that God would help them. Even though you may not be guilty of the same sins as Limhi's people, how can his words help you turn to the Lord? You will notice, for example, that Limhi reminded his people about past accounts of God's deliverance (see verses 18–20). How do these accounts, as well as other scriptural accounts or personal experiences, help you trust God?

What were the 24 plates found by Limhi's people?

While a small group of Limhi's people were searching unsuccessfully for the land of Zarahemla, they found 24 plates of gold with engravings in an unfamiliar language. These plates, which were eventually translated by King Mosiah, told of a people known as the Jaredites, who came to the promised land from the Tower of Babel and were eventually destroyed (see Mosiah 28:11–19). Later Moroni made an abridgment of these plates (see Ether 1:1–2), which became the book of Ether. Note in Mosiah 28:18 the effect of this record on Mosiah's people.

The Lord provides prophets, seers, and revelators to benefit mankind.

When Limhi heard Ammon's testimony that the Lord had raised up a seer, Limhi "rejoiced exceedingly, and gave thanks to God" (Mosiah 8:19). Why do you suppose he felt that way? What do you learn about seers from Ammon's words in Mosiah 8:13–19? In our day, "the First Presidency and the Council of the Twelve are sustained as prophets, seers, and revelators" (Bible Dictionary, "Seer"). When was the last time you pondered the blessing of having prophets, seers, and revelators on the earth? Perhaps you could record how prophets, seers, and revelators have been a "great benefit" to you (Mosiah 8:18).

The Prophet Joseph Smith is the great seer who stands at the head of our dispensation (see D&C 21:1; 124:125; Joseph Smith—History 1:62). How did he exemplify Ammon's description of a seer during his ministry?

I can face my challenges "in the strength of the Lord."

Zeniff admitted that he had made mistakes. He was overzealous at times, and he had put his people—the ancestors of Limhi's people—in a difficult situation by making an ill-advised agreement with King Laman. But later, when he went to battle against the Lamanites, he helped his people face their challenges with faith. As you read Mosiah 9–10, look for what Zeniff's people did to show their faith. How did God strengthen them? What does it mean to you to go forth "in the strength of the Lord"? (Mosiah 9:17; 10:10–11).

MOSIAH 10:11–17

My choices can influence generations.

According to Mosiah 10:11–17, how did the actions and attitudes of the Lamanites' ancestors prevent the Lamanites from knowing the truth? How did the choices of the Lamanites' ancestors affect future generations? Think about the people who might be influenced by your beliefs and choices; what are you doing to help them more fully have faith in Christ?

Ideas for Family Scripture Study and Family Home Evening

As you read the scriptures with your family, the Spirit can help you know what principles to emphasize and discuss in order to meet the needs of your family. Here are some ideas.

Mosiah 7:19–20. Note the examples that Limhi pointed to in order to encourage his people to have faith. What examples from the scriptures inspire us to "trust in God"? What does it mean to put our trust in God? (see also Mosiah 9:17; 10:19). What stories from our lives or our ancestors' lives can we share to inspire greater trust in God?

Mosiah 7:26–27. What do we learn about the Savior from these verses? (see also D&C 130:22). Why are we grateful to know these things?

Mosiah 8:13–18. To help family members understand what a seer is, perhaps you could show them pictures of tools that help us see things we couldn't otherwise see, such as binoculars, a telescope, or a microscope. How are these tools like a seer? (see Moses 6:35–36). What can seers see that we do not? What evidence do we have that Joseph Smith was a seer?

You might show pictures of our living prophets, seers, and revelators and ask your family what they know about them. How are we following them?

Mosiah 9:14–18; 10:1–10. When the Lamanites attacked, the people of Zeniff were physically and spiritually ready. What can we learn from Zeniff and his people about preparing for challenges?

For more ideas for teaching children, see this week's outline in *Come, Follow Me—For Primary*.

Improving Personal Study

Seek your own spiritual insights. This outline suggests passages and principles to focus on, but don't let these suggestions limit your study. You might be impressed by verses or discover principles not mentioned here. Let the Spirit guide you.

Vision to Joseph Smith, by Clark Kelley Price

Abinadi before King Noah, by Andrew Bosley

Mosiah 11–17

"A LIGHT . . . THAT CAN NEVER BE DARKENED"

Abinadi's words caused a mighty change in at least one member of King Noah's court (see Mosiah 17:2–4). Read Mosiah 11–17 with a prayer in your heart that you will receive impressions about how you can change.

RECORD YOUR IMPRESSIONS

Large fires can start from a single spark. Abinadi was only one man testifying against a powerful king and his court. His words were rejected for the most part, and he was sentenced to death. Yet his testimony of Jesus Christ, who is the "light . . . that can never be darkened" (Mosiah 16:9), sparked something inside the young priest Alma. And that spark of conversion slowly grew as Alma brought many others to repentance and faith in Jesus Christ. The flames that killed Abinadi eventually died out, but the fire of faith that his words created would have a lasting influence on the Nephites—and on those who read his words today. Most of us will never face quite what Abinadi did because of our testimonies, but we all have moments when following Jesus Christ is a test of our courage and faith. Perhaps studying Abinadi's testimony will fan the flames of testimony and courage in your heart as well.

Ideas for Personal Scripture Study

MOSIAH 11–13; 17

I can stand for truth, even when I stand alone.

Imagine how discouraging it must have been for Abinadi to cry repentance to a people who did not seem at all interested in changing their wicked ways. His message was rejected again and again. Yet Abinadi never gave up.

When have you felt like you were standing alone in defense of the truth? As you read Mosiah 11–13 and 17, what do you learn that can help you be ready when the Lord needs you to stand up for His gospel? What other principles do you learn from Abinadi's example?

MOSIAH 12:19–30

I need to apply my heart to understanding God's word.

King Noah's priests were familiar with the word of God—they could quote passages of scripture and claimed to teach the commandments. But those commandments were "not written in [their] hearts," and they had "not applied [their] hearts to understanding" them (Mosiah 13:11; 12:27). As a result, their lives remained unchanged.

As you read Mosiah 12:19–30, ponder what it means to apply your heart to understanding God's word. Does this inspire you to make any changes in the way you approach learning the gospel?

MOSIAH 13:1–9

The Lord will sustain His servants in His work.

On the one hand, Abinadi's experience gives multiple examples of how the Lord supports His servants—

you can find several such examples in Mosiah 13:1–9. On the other hand, the Lord also allowed Abinadi to be persecuted, imprisoned, and martyred for his testimony. What do you find in these verses that reveals that Abinadi trusted the Lord? How does Abinadi's example affect the way you view your callings and responsibilities?

MOSIAH 14–15

Jesus Christ suffered for me.

King Noah and his priests believed that salvation came through the law of Moses. Abinadi wanted them to know that salvation comes through the Messiah, Jesus Christ. In Mosiah 14–15, notice words and phrases that describe the Savior and what He suffered for you. What verses help deepen your love and gratitude toward Him?

MOSIAH 15:1–12

How is Jesus Christ both the Father and the Son?

These passages are sometimes confusing because it can seem that Abinadi is teaching that Heavenly Father and Jesus Christ are the same Being, yet we know that they are separate Beings. What did Abinadi mean? He taught that God the Son—Jehovah—would be the Redeemer (see Mosiah 15:1), dwelling in the flesh, becoming part man and part God (verses 2–3). He completely subjected Himself to the will of God the Father (verses 5–9). Because of this, Jesus Christ is both the Son of God and the perfect earthly representation of God the Father (see John 14:6–10).

Abinadi continued by explaining that Jesus Christ is also the Father in the sense that when we accept His redemption, we become "his seed" (Mosiah 15:11–12). In other words, we become spiritually reborn through Him (see Mosiah 5:7).

See also John 5:25–27; 8:28–29; 17:20–23; "The Father and the Son," *Ensign,* Apr. 2002, 12–18.

Ideas for Family Scripture Study and Family Home Evening

As you read the scriptures with your family, the Spirit can help you know what principles to emphasize and discuss in order to meet the needs of your family. Here are some ideas.

Mosiah 11–13; 17. Abinadi and Alma are inspiring examples of staying loyal to the truth even when doing so is unpopular. Members of your family may be facing social pressure to compromise their standards. What can they learn from Abinadi and Alma about standing for truth? The artwork accompanying this outline could help your family visualize the account. After studying these chapters, consider role-playing real-life scenarios so that your family members can practice responding to pressure to compromise their standards. Or you could share with each other experiences you've had standing for truth.

Mosiah 12:33–37; 13:11–24. What does it mean to have God's commandments "written in [our] hearts"? (Mosiah 13:11). Maybe you could write some ideas (or draw pictures of your ideas) on a large heart-shaped paper. Why are the commandments precious to us? How can we write them in our hearts?

Studying the scriptures can help us write the commandments in our hearts.

Mosiah 14. In this chapter you will find several words and phrases that describe Jesus Christ. Maybe your family could list them as you find them. How do family members feel about the Savior as we study these words and phrases?

Mosiah 15:26–27; 16:1–13. These verses describe what would happen to God's children if Jesus had "not come into the world" (Mosiah 16:6) or if they did not follow Him. What are the good things that have happened because He came and atoned for us? See also the video "Why We Need a Savior" (ChurchofJesusChrist.org).

For more ideas for teaching children, see this week's outline in *Come, Follow Me—For Primary.*

Improving Our Teaching

Use stories and examples to teach gospel principles. The Savior often taught gospel principles using stories and parables. Think of examples and stories from your own life that can make a gospel principle come alive for your family (see *Teaching in the Savior's Way,* 22).

His Face Shone with Exceeding Luster, by Jeremy Winborg

Minerva Teichert (1888–1976), Escape of King Limhi and His People, 1949–1951, oil on masonite, 35 7/8 x 48 inches. Brigham Young University Museum of Art, 1969.

MAY 11–17

Mosiah 18–24

WE HAVE ENTERED INTO A COVENANT WITH HIM

President Thomas S. Monson taught, "As we read and ponder the scriptures, we will experience the sweet whisperings of the Spirit to our souls" ("We Never Walk Alone," *Ensign* or *Liahona,* Nov. 2013, 122).

RECORD YOUR IMPRESSIONS_____

_____

_____

The account of Alma and his people in Mosiah 18; 23–24 shows what it means to "come into the fold of God" (Mosiah 18:8). When they were baptized, they made a covenant with God to "serve him and keep his commandments" (Mosiah 18:10). While this was an intensely personal commitment, it also had to do with how they treated one another. Yes, the journey back to Heavenly Father is personal and individual, and no one can keep our covenants for us, but that doesn't mean we are alone. We need each other.

As members of Christ's Church, we covenant to serve God by helping and serving one another along the way, "bear[ing] one another's burdens" (Mosiah 18:8–10). Alma's people definitely had burdens to bear, just as we all do. And one way the Lord helps us "bear up [our] burdens with ease" (Mosiah 24:15) is by giving us a community of Saints who have promised to mourn with us and comfort us, just as we have promised to do for them.

Ideas for Personal Scripture Study

MOSIAH 18:1–17

Baptism includes a covenant to serve God and stand as a witness of Him.

Mosiah 18:8–10 contains Alma's teachings about the baptismal covenant, or the promise we make to God at baptism. As you read these verses, ponder the following questions:

- What do you learn from these verses about the promises you made at baptism? What does God promise you?

- How does the covenant to serve God (see verse 10) relate to our efforts to minister to one another? (see verses 8–9).

- What are you doing to keep your promises?

- How does keeping your baptismal covenant help you be "filled with the Spirit"? (Mosiah 18:14). How does the Spirit help you keep your covenant?

When I make covenants with God, I receive His blessings.

This account also reveals the proper mode of baptism. What do you learn in verses 14–17 about how baptism should be performed? What else do you learn about baptism from Matthew 3:16; Romans 6:3–5; 3 Nephi 11:21–28; and Doctrine and Covenants 20:72–74?

See also Doctrine and Covenants 20:37, 77, 79.

MOSIAH 18:17–30

God's people should be united.

As Alma and his people discovered, following Jesus Christ sometimes means leaving a familiar way of life for something new and different. But Alma's people drew strength from each other as part of "the church of Christ" (Mosiah 18:17). How do the teachings in Mosiah 18:17–30 inspire you to be a better member of the Church? What can you do to help your ward or branch members be "knit together in unity and in love"? (Mosiah 18:21).

See also Henry B. Eyring, "Our Hearts Knit as One," *Ensign* or *Liahona,* Nov. 2008, 68–71.

MOSIAH 19–20

The words of the prophets will be fulfilled.

Abinadi made some specific prophecies about what would happen to King Noah and his people if they refused to repent. However, to some these prophecies seemed unbelievable (see Mosiah 12:1–8, 14–15), especially since the Nephites had successfully defended themselves against the Lamanites for nearly 50 years (see Mosiah 9:16–18; 11:19). But the words of the prophets will all be fulfilled—in our day as much as in Abinadi's.

What do you find in Mosiah 19–20 that would lead Gideon to declare that Abinadi's prophecies had been fulfilled? (see Mosiah 20:21). How does this account strengthen your faith in the warnings and counsel of God's prophets and your commitment to follow their words? When have you seen a prophet's words fulfilled in our day?

MOSIAH 21–24

God can make my burdens light.

Limhi's people and Alma's people both fell into bondage, although for different reasons and in different circumstances. What can you learn by comparing the accounts of Limhi's people in Mosiah 19–22 and Alma's people in Mosiah 18; 23–24? You could note how each of these groups responded to captivity or how each was eventually delivered. As you do, look for messages that apply to your life. For example, what do you learn from these accounts that will help you carry your burdens?

MOSIAH 23:21–24; 24:8–17

I can trust the Lord.

Even though they had repented of their sins, Alma and his people still found themselves in bondage. Their experience shows that trusting the Lord and living our covenants doesn't always prevent difficulties, but it does help us overcome them. As you read Mosiah 23:21–24 and 24:8–17, note words and phrases that can help you learn to trust in God, regardless of your circumstances.

See also Thomas S. Monson, "I Will Not Fail Thee, nor Forsake Thee," *Ensign* or *Liahona,* Nov. 2013, 85–87.

Ideas for Family Scripture Study and Family Home Evening

As you read the scriptures with your family, the Spirit can help you know what principles to emphasize and discuss in order to meet the needs of your family. Here are some ideas.

Mosiah 18:1–4. There is a saying that you can count the seeds in an apple, but you can't count the apples that come from one seed. Only one person was receptive to Abinadi's testimony, but that one person—Alma—influenced generations of Nephites. Perhaps you could use a fruit with seeds to demonstrate this principle. How does this message apply to our family? What can we do to share our testimonies with others?

Mosiah 18:8–10. What can we learn about our baptismal covenant from these verses? (see also D&C 20:73, 77–79). What are we doing to prepare for or keep our baptismal covenant?

Mosiah 18:30. What places have special meaning to us because of the spiritual experiences we had there?

Mosiah 21:11–16; 24:10–15. What do we learn by comparing the captivity of Alma's people and Limhi's people?

Mosiah 21:15; 24:11–15. What do these verses teach us about some of the ways the Lord answers prayers?

For more ideas for teaching children, see this week's outline in *Come, Follow Me—For Primary.*

Improving Personal Study

Find a time that works for you. It is often easiest to learn when you can study the scriptures without being interrupted. Find a time that works for you, and do your best to consistently study at that time each day.

The Waters of Mormon, by Jorge Cocco

Conversion of Alma the Younger, by Gary L. Kapp

Mosiah 25–28

"THEY WERE CALLED THE PEOPLE OF GOD"

After "the voice of the Lord came to [Alma]," he wrote down the things the Lord told him "that he might have them" (Mosiah 26:14, 33). How will you follow Alma's example?

RECORD YOUR IMPRESSIONS

After nearly three generations of living in separate lands, the Nephites were one people again. Limhi's people, Alma's people, and Mosiah's people—even the people of Zarahemla, who were not descended from Nephi—were now all "numbered with the Nephites" (Mosiah 25:13). Many of them also wanted to become members of the Church that Alma had established. So all those who "were desirous to take upon them the name of Christ" were baptized, "and they were called the people of God" (Mosiah 25:23–24). After years of conflict and captivity, it seemed that the Nephites would finally enjoy a period of peace.

But before long, unbelievers began persecuting the Saints. What made this especially heartbreaking was that many of these unbelievers were the believers' own children—the "rising generation" (Mosiah 26:1), including the sons of Mosiah and one son of Alma. Then a miracle happened, and the account of that miracle has given hope to anguished parents for generations. But the story of Alma's conversion is not just for parents of wayward children. True conversion is a miracle that, in one way or another, needs to happen in all of us.

Ideas for Personal Scripture Study

MOSIAH 26:1–6

I am responsible for my own faith and testimony.

Those who heard King Benjamin's sermon experienced a marvelous conversion (see Mosiah 5:1–7), but conversion is a personal experience that cannot be passed along like an inheritance to one's children. We all must experience our own conversion to the gospel of Jesus Christ. As you read in Mosiah 26:1–6 about "the rising generation" of unbelieving Nephites, note the consequences of their unbelief. You might also think about people whom you wish you could bring to Christ. While you can't give them your conversion, the Spirit may whisper things you *can* do to help them find faith. As you read in Mosiah 25–28 about how Alma and other Church members helped the rising generation, additional thoughts might come to you.

See also Doctrine and Covenants 68:25–29.

MOSIAH 26:6–39

God's faithful servants seek to do His will.

Sometimes we might think that a Church leader like Alma always knows the right thing to do. In Mosiah 26 we read of a problem in the Church that Alma had never dealt with, and "he feared that he should do wrong in the sight of God" (Mosiah 26:13). What did Alma do in this situation? (see Mosiah 26:13–14, 33–34, 38–39). What does Alma's experience suggest about how you might approach difficult problems in your family or your Church service?

It might also be interesting to list the truths that God revealed to Alma, found in Mosiah 26:15–32. Notice that some of these truths were not in direct response to Alma's question. What does this suggest to you about prayer and receiving personal revelation?

MOSIAH 27:8–37

All men and women must be born again.

It was obvious that Alma the Younger needed a spiritual rebirth, for he and the sons of Mosiah were "the very vilest of sinners," who went about "to destroy the church of God" (Mosiah 28:4; 27:10). But soon after his conversion, Alma testified that conversion is available—and essential—for everyone: "Marvel not," he said, "that *all* mankind . . . must be born again" (Mosiah 27:25; italics added). That, of course, includes you.

His Father Rejoiced, by Walter Rane

As you read about Alma's experience, found in Mosiah 27:8–37, you might try putting yourself in his place. You aren't trying to destroy the Church, but you can surely think of things about yourself that need to change. Who, like Alma's father, is supporting you and praying for you "with much faith"? What experiences have helped "convince [you] of the power and authority of God"? (Mosiah 27:14). What "great things" has the Lord done for you or your family that you should "remember"? (Mosiah 27:16). What do you learn from Alma the Younger's words and actions about what it means to be born again? Questions like these might help you evaluate your progress in the process of being born again.

See also Mosiah 5:6–9; Alma 36; "Conversion," Gospel Topics, topics.ChurchofJesusChrist.org.

MOSIAH 27:14, 19–24

God hears my prayers and will answer them according to His will.

Maybe you know a parent in Alma the Elder's situation, whose son or daughter is making destructive choices. Or maybe you are that parent. What do you find in Mosiah 27:14, 19–24 that gives you hope? How might these verses influence your prayers in behalf of others?

Ideas for Family Scripture Study and Family Home Evening

As you read the scriptures with your family, the Spirit can help you know what principles to emphasize and discuss in order to meet the needs of your family. Here are some ideas.

Mosiah 25:5–11. How did Mosiah's people feel after he read to them the records of Zeniff's people and Alma's people? Has your family kept any records you could read from? Maybe you could add to your records or start keeping your own. What would you include that might help your family (including future generations) be "filled with exceedingly great joy" and learn about "the immediate goodness of God"? (Mosiah 25:8, 10).

Mosiah 25:16. Why was it important for Limhi's people to remember that the Lord had delivered them out of captivity? What has the Lord done for us that we should remember?

Mosiah 26:29–31; 27:35. According to these verses, what must a person do to receive forgiveness?

Mosiah 27:21–24. As you read these verses, consider someone your family could pray and fast for.

Mosiah 27–28. To help your family visualize the accounts in these chapters, you might invite them to draw pictures of the people involved and use the pictures to retell the story. Or they might enjoy acting out the story; how could they portray the change that Alma and the sons of Mosiah experienced?

For more ideas for teaching children, see this week's outline in *Come, Follow Me—For Primary.*

Improving Our Teaching

Use art. The *Gospel Art Book* and the Media Library on ChurchofJesusChrist.org contain many images and videos that can help your family visualize concepts or events."

Illustration of an angel appearing to Alma the Younger by Kevin Keele

Alma the Younger Preaching, by Gary L. Kapp

Mosiah 29–Alma 4

"THEY WERE STEADFAST AND IMMOVABLE"

Reading the scriptures invites revelation. Be open to the messages the Lord wants to give you.

RECORD YOUR IMPRESSIONS

Some might see King Mosiah's proposal to replace kings with elected judges as merely wise political reform. But to the Nephites, especially those who lived under wicked King Noah, this change had spiritual significance too. They had seen how an unrighteous king had caused "iniquity" and "great destruction" among his people (Mosiah 29:17), and they were "exceedingly anxious" to be free from such influence. This change would allow them to be responsible for their own righteousness and "answer for [their] own sins" (Mosiah 29:38; see also D&C 101:78).

Of course, the end of the reign of kings did not mean the end of problems in Nephite society. Cunning people like Nehor and Amlici promoted false ideas, nonbelievers persecuted the Saints, and many members of the Church became prideful and fell away. Yet "the humble followers of God" remained "steadfast and immovable" despite what happened around them (Alma 1:25). And because of the change enacted by Mosiah, they could "cast in their voices" to influence their society for good (Alma 2:6).

Ideas for Personal Scripture Study

MOSIAH 29:11–27; ALMA 2:1–7

I can be a positive influence in my community.

Just five years into the reign of the judges, a crisis arose that would test Mosiah's declaration that the voice of the people would usually choose what was right (see Mosiah 29:26). The issue involved religious freedom: a man named Amlici sought to "deprive [the people] of their rights and privileges of the church" (Alma 2:4). Have you noticed religious rights being threatened in your nation or community? What do you learn from the way the Nephites responded to this threat? (see Alma 2:1–7).

There are likely many important issues facing your community. How can you, like the Nephites, make sure that your voice is included in "the voice of the people"? Perhaps you live in a place where the voice of the people has limited influence on the government; if so, are there other ways you can be a positive influence in your community?

ALMA 1

I can recognize and reject false doctrine.

Although Nehor eventually confessed that what he taught was false, his teachings continued to influence the Nephites for many years (see Alma 1:15–16; 2:1–2; 14:14–18; 15:15; 21:4; 24:28). Why might people have found Nehor's teachings enticing? As you read Alma 1:2–4, see if you can identify the falsehoods in Nehor's teachings; you'll probably notice that they're taught alongside partial truths.

Gideon withstood Nehor "with the words of God" (Alma 1:7, 9). Can you think of scriptures that refute Nehor's falsehoods? Here are some examples, but there are many others: Matthew 7:21–23; 2 Nephi 26:29–31; Mosiah 18:24–26; and Helaman 12:25–26. How can these scriptures help you refute falsehoods taught today?

Another way to approach your study of Alma 1 is to compare Nehor and his followers (verses 3–9, 16–20) with "the people of God" (verses 25–30; see also 2 Nephi 26:29–31). How can you be more like the people of God? Do you notice any "priestcraft" in your own service?

ALMA 1:27–31; 4:6–15

True disciples of Jesus Christ do not set their hearts upon riches.

Chapters 1 and 4 of Alma both describe periods when the Church prospered, but Church members responded to that prosperity differently in each case. What differences do you notice? Based on what you find, how would you describe the attitude that "humble followers of God" (Alma 4:15) have toward riches and prosperity? What do you feel inspired to change about your own attitude?

ALMA 4

The "word of God" and "pure testimony" can change hearts.

What made Alma "very sorrowful" (Alma 4:15) in Alma 4? Some might say that the office of chief judge would have put Alma in the best position to solve the problems he saw among his people. But Alma felt there was a better way. What impresses you about his approach to helping his people? Your study may inspire thoughts about how you can righteously influence those around you; if so, act on those thoughts.

Ideas for Family Scripture Study and Family Home Evening

As you read the scriptures with your family, the Spirit can help you know what principles to emphasize and discuss in order to meet the needs of your family. Here are some ideas.

Alma 1:19–25. Your family might benefit from identifying the different ways Church members responded to persecution in these verses. Maybe you could practice ways to respond appropriately when others attack our beliefs. The videos at ChurchofJesusChrist.org/religious-freedom/examples might help.

Alma 3:4. What message did the Amlicites want to communicate when they "set [a] mark upon themselves"? (see Alma 3:4, 13). What messages might we send—intentionally or unintentionally—with our appearance? This might be a good time to review "Dress and Appearance" in *For the Strength of Youth* (2011), 6–8.

Alma 4:2–3. What things or experiences have "awakened [us] to a remembrance of [our] duty" toward God? (Alma 4:3). Maybe it would be effective to share these verses after waking your family in the morning. You might then discuss how the challenges of waking up physically help us understand the challenges of waking up spiritually.

Alma 4:10–11. How can we avoid being a "stumbling-block to those who [do] not belong to the church"? (Alma 4:10). It might also be useful to talk about how we can make sure the actions of others, particularly fellow Church members, do not become stumbling blocks for our spiritual progress.

Alma 4:19. To help your family understand the power of testimony, you could ask them to think of a time when hearing someone's testimony affected them deeply. Why might Alma have chosen to use testimony and the word of God to touch the hearts of the people? (see also Alma 31:5). Why is this more effective than other methods people might use to persuade others to change? Are there people whose faith we could strengthen by sharing our testimonies with them?

For more ideas for teaching children, see this week's outline in *Come, Follow Me—For Primary.*

Improving Personal Study

Liken the scriptures to yourself. Consider how the stories and teachings of the scriptures apply to your life. For example, you might find parallels between today's world and the societal problems the Nephites faced in Alma 1–4.

Alma and Amlici, by Scott M. Snow

Ye Are Not Forgotten, by Jon McNaughton

JUNE 1–7

Alma 5–7

"HAVE YE EXPERIENCED THIS MIGHTY CHANGE IN YOUR HEARTS?"

Alma 5–7 can help you reflect on your ongoing conversion to Jesus Christ. As you read, record what the Spirit teaches you.

RECORD YOUR IMPRESSIONS _____

_____

_____

Alma did not know about today's lifesaving heart transplant surgeries, which replace a damaged or diseased heart with a healthy one. But he knew about a more miraculous "change of heart" (Alma 5:26)—one whereby the Savior gives us a newness of spiritual life, like being "born again" (see Alma 5:14, 49). Alma could see that this change of heart was exactly what many of the Nephites needed. Some were rich and others poor, some prideful and others humble, some persecutors and others afflicted by persecution (see Alma 4:6–15). But all of them needed to come unto Jesus Christ to be healed—just as we all do. Whether we are seeking to overcome pride or to endure afflictions, Alma's message is the same: "Come and fear not" (Alma 7:15). Let the Savior change a hardened, sinful, or wounded heart into one that is humble, pure, and new.

Ideas for Personal Scripture Study

I must experience—and continue to feel—a mighty change of heart.

The introspective questions that Alma asked the people of Zarahemla, found in Alma 5:14–33, can help you search your own soul and understand what it means to experience a "mighty change of heart" throughout your life. President M. Russell Ballard explained the value of these questions: "I need to regularly take time to ask myself, 'How am I doing?' It's kind of like having a personal, private interview with yourself. . . . As a guide for me during this private, personal review, I like to read and ponder the introspective words found in the fifth chapter of Alma" ("Return and Receive," *Ensign* or *Liahona,* May 2017, 64).

Each disciple of Christ must experience a "change of heart."

Consider reading Alma's questions as if you were interviewing yourself and examining your heart. You may want to record your responses to the questions. What do you feel inspired to do as a result of your interview?

See also Dale G. Renlund, "Preserving the Heart's Mighty Change," *Ensign* or *Liahona,* Nov. 2009, 97–99.

I can gain my own witness of the Savior and His gospel through the Holy Ghost.

Alma bore powerful testimony of the Savior and His gospel, and he also explained how he gained that testimony. As he testified, he did not mention his experience with seeing and hearing an angel (see Mosiah 27:10–17) but rather described the price he paid to know the truth for himself. What do you learn from Alma 5:44–51 about how Alma came to know the truth? How can you follow his example in your efforts to gain or strengthen your testimony? What do you learn about the Savior from Alma's teachings in Alma 5:33–35, 48–50, and 57–60?

Diligent obedience will help me stay on the "path which leads to the kingdom of God."

The people of Gideon were not struggling with the same dilemmas as the people in Zarahemla, so the Spirit helped Alma perceive their needs and teach them differently (see Alma 7:17, 26). You might notice some differences between Alma's messages in Zarahemla (see Alma 5) and in Gideon (see Alma 7). For example, Alma perceived that the people of Gideon were "in the path which leads to the kingdom of God" (Alma 7:19). Throughout his sermon to them, Alma taught them many things about how to stay on that path (see Alma 7). What counsel did he give them? What can you apply to your life now?

The Savior took upon Himself my sins, pains, and afflictions.

Have you ever felt that no one understands your struggles or challenges? If so, the truths taught in Alma 7:7–16 can help. Elder David A. Bednar testified: "The Son of God perfectly knows and understands, for He has felt and borne our individual burdens. And because of His infinite and eternal sacrifice (see Alma 34:14), He has perfect empathy and can extend to us His arm of mercy" ("Bear Up Their Burdens with Ease," *Ensign* or *Liahona,* May 2014, 90).

As you read Alma 7:7–16, reflect on what these verses help us understand about the purposes of the Savior's sacrifice. How do we access His power in our lives? Consider recording your thoughts.

See also Isaiah 53:3–5.

Ideas for Family Scripture Study and Family Home Evening

As you read the scriptures with your family, the Spirit can help you know what principles to emphasize and discuss in order to meet the needs of your family. Here are some ideas.

Alma 5:6–13. Why did Alma want his people to remember the Lord's mercy toward their ancestors? What stories from your family history teach you about His mercy? Maybe you could visit familysearch.org/myfamily to record these stories.

Alma 5:14–33. Members of your family may know what it feels like to be prepared—or unprepared—for a camping trip, a test at school, or a job interview. What recent experiences could they share to illustrate the importance of being prepared? You could invite family members to review Alma 5:14–33 and find questions Alma asked to prepare his people to meet God. Perhaps each family member could choose a question and share how it can help us prepare to meet God. Your family could also display several of Alma's questions around your home for family members to ponder.

Alma 6:4–6. What are some of the reasons we gather as Saints? How can we make our time at church more helpful to ourselves and others?

Alma 7:9–16. What do we learn in these verses that helps us "fear not" (Alma 7:15) when we need to repent and change? What do these verses teach us about turning to the Savior when we need help? What other things have we done to receive His help? How has He succored us?

Alma 7:23. Who do we know who is a good example of one or more of the qualities listed in this verse? Why is it important to develop these qualities?

For more ideas for teaching children, see this week's outline in *Come, Follow Me—For Primary.*

Improving Our Teaching

Ask questions that invite family members to act. Consider questions that prompt your family members to reflect on how they can live the gospel more fully. "These are usually not discussion questions; they are for personal reflection" (*Teaching in the Savior's Way,* 31).

Our Advocate, by Jay Bryant Ward

Teaching True Doctrine, by Michael T. Malm

Alma 8–12

JESUS CHRIST WILL COME TO REDEEM HIS PEOPLE

Studying the scriptures invites revelation. So as you read Alma 8–12, record the impressions of the Spirit as He teaches you from the messages of Alma and Amulek.

RECORD YOUR IMPRESSIONS

God's work will not fail. But our efforts to help with His work sometimes seem to fail—at least, we may not immediately see the outcomes we hope for. At times we might feel a little like Alma when he preached the gospel in Ammonihah—rejected, spit on, and cast out. Yet when an angel instructed him to go back and try again, Alma courageously "returned speedily" (Alma 8:18), and God prepared the way before him. Not only did He provide Alma food to eat and a place to stay, but He also prepared Amulek, who became a fellow laborer, a fierce defender of the gospel, and a faithful friend. When we face setbacks and disappointments as we serve in the Lord's kingdom, we can remember how God supported and led Alma, and we can trust that God will support and lead us too, even in difficult circumstances.

Ideas for Personal Scripture Study

ALMA 8

My efforts to share the gospel may require persistence and patience.

Even though someone may reject your testimony of the gospel, that doesn't mean you should lose hope—after all, the Lord won't give up on that person, and He will guide you in how to act. In Alma's case, an angel commanded him to return to Ammonihah to preach the gospel even though the people there had already violently rejected him (see Alma 8:14–16). What do you learn from Alma's example of sharing the gospel despite challenges and opposition? Which verses in Alma 8 increase your desire to share the gospel?

See also 3 Nephi 18:30–32; Jeffrey R. Holland, "The Cost—and Blessings—of Discipleship," *Ensign* or *Liahona,* May 2014, 6–9.

ALMA 9:18–25; 10:16–23

God judges His children according to the light and knowledge they have.

When reading about the way the Nephites in Ammonihah treated the Lord's servants, it is easy to forget that they were once a gospel-living and "highly favored people of the Lord" (Alma 9:20). In fact, part of Alma's message to the people in Ammonihah was that because they had hardened their hearts despite being so richly blessed, their state was worse than that of the Lamanites, who sinned mostly in ignorance. What does this contrast teach us about how God judges His children?

As you read about the great blessings God gave the people of Nephi (see especially Alma 9:19–23), ponder the great blessings He has given you. What

are you doing to stay true to these blessings? What changes do you feel you need to make?

See also Doctrine and Covenants 82:3.

ALMA 11–12

God's plan is a plan of redemption.

Book of Mormon prophets used a variety of names to describe God's plan for His children, like the plan of salvation or the plan of happiness. In Alma 11–12, Alma and Amulek referred to it as the plan of redemption. As you read these chapters, ponder why the word "redemption" is used to describe the plan. You could also write a short summary of what Alma and Amulek taught about the following aspects of the plan.

The Fall:

The Redeemer:

Repentance:

Death:

Resurrection:

Judgment:

Notice the effect Amulek's words had on the people (see Alma 11:46). Why do you think these principles had such a powerful influence? How have they influenced your life?

See also D. Todd Christofferson, "The Resurrection of Jesus Christ," *Ensign* or *Liahona,* May 2014, 111–14.

ALMA 12:8–18

If I will not harden my heart, I can receive more of the word of God.

Some people may wonder why Heavenly Father doesn't make everything known to us. In Alma 12:9–14, Alma explained one possible reason God's mysteries are sometimes withheld from us. These questions could help you ponder what he taught:

- What does it mean to harden our hearts? Do you ever notice this tendency in yourself?

- Why might the Lord withhold His word from those who have hardened their hearts?

- How have you experienced the promise of receiving a "greater portion of the word"? (Alma 12:10). What was that experience like?

- What can you do to ensure that God's word is "found in [you]"? (Alma 12:13). If you had God's word in you, what effect would it have on your "words," "works," and "thoughts"? (Alma 12:14).

For an example of these principles, compare Amulek to the other people of Ammonihah. How does Amulek's experience (see especially Alma 10:1–11) illustrate what Alma taught in these verses?

Ideas for Family Scripture Study and Family Home Evening

As you read the scriptures with your family, the Spirit can help you know what principles to emphasize and discuss in order to meet the needs of your family. Here are some ideas.

Alma 8:10–18. What can we learn from Alma about obeying the Lord "speedily" (verse 18) even when it might be difficult? To reinforce this principle with small children, you could play a game where you give instructions for a task and see how quickly family members accomplish it. For instance, you might see who could quickly fold a piece of clothing.

Alma 10:1–12. What can we learn from Amulek's experience in these verses? What effect did his testimony have on those listening? Invite your family members to make a plan to do one thing this week based on what they learned from Amulek's example.

Alma 10:22–23. What do we learn from these verses about the influence a group of righteous people can have in a wicked city?

Alma 11:34–37. What is the difference between Jesus Christ saving us *in* our sins and *from* our sins? (see Helaman 5:10; see also 1 John 1:9–10). To illustrate what Amulek taught, you might share the story at the beginning of Elder Allen D. Haynie's message "Remembering in Whom We Have Trusted" (*Ensign* or *Liahona,* Nov. 2015, 121–23). How does Jesus Christ save us from our sins?

For more ideas for teaching children, see this week's outline in *Come, Follow Me—For Primary.*

Improving Personal Study

Study the words of latter-day prophets and apostles. Read what latter-day prophets and apostles have taught about the truths you find in the scriptures. For instance, you could identify a topic in Alma 8–12 and look for that topic in the most recent general conference (see *Teaching in the Savior's Way,* 21).

Illustration of Alma eating with Amulek by Dan Burr

Illustration of Alma and Amulek being delivered from prison, by Andrew Bosley

Alma 13–16

"ENTER INTO THE REST OF THE LORD"

The inspiration you receive as you ponder the scriptures is precious. You can show that you treasure it by recording and acting on it.

RECORD YOUR IMPRESSIONS

In many ways, life in Ammonihah had been good for both Amulek and Zeezrom. Amulek was "a man of no small reputation," with "many kindreds and friends" and "much riches" (Alma 10:4). Zeezrom was "one of the most expert" among the lawyers and enjoyed "much business" (Alma 10:31). Then Alma arrived in Ammonihah with a divine invitation to repent and "enter into the rest of the Lord" (Alma 13:16). For Amulek, Zeezrom, and others, accepting this invitation required sacrifice and even led to almost unbearable adversity.

But of course the story doesn't end there. In Alma 13–16, we learn what ultimately happens to those who believe "in the power of Christ unto salvation" (Alma 15:6). Sometimes there's deliverance, sometimes healing—and sometimes things don't get any easier in this life. But always, "the Lord receiveth [His people] up unto himself, in glory" (Alma 14:11). Always, the Lord grants "power, according to [our] faith which [is] in Christ" (Alma 14:28). And always, that "faith on the Lord" gives us "hope that [we] shall receive eternal life" (Alma 13:29). As you read these chapters, you can take comfort in these promises, and you may come to understand better what Alma meant when he spoke of "the rest of the Lord."

Ideas for Personal Scripture Study

ALMA 13:1–19

Priesthood ordinances help me receive redemption through Jesus Christ.

You might recall that in Alma 12, Alma taught about God's plan of redemption (see Alma 12:24–27). In chapter 13, he spoke about the priests whom God ordained "to teach these things unto the people" (Alma 13:1). Alma's words reveal many powerful truths about the priesthood. Perhaps you could try to identify at least one truth per verse in Alma 13:1–9. Here are some ideas to get you started:

Verse 1. The priesthood is also called "the order of [God's] Son" (see also D&C 107:1–4).

Verse 2. God ordains priests to help people look to His Son for redemption.

Verse 3. Priesthood holders were prepared for their responsibilities "from the foundation of the world."

What else do you find? How do you feel about the priesthood as you ponder these truths? How have priesthood ordinances helped you look to Christ for redemption?

Priesthood ordinances help us look to Jesus Christ for redemption.

It's interesting to note that many of the people in Ammonihah were followers of Nehor (see Alma 14:18; 15:15). How were priests of Nehor's order (see Alma 1:3–6) different from the priests ordained "after the Order of the Son of God" (D&C 107:3), whom Alma described? (see Alma 13:1–19).

See also Dale G. Renlund, "The Priesthood and the Savior's Atoning Power," *Ensign* or *Liahona*, Nov. 2017, 64–67.

ALMA 13:3

Are priesthood holders the only people "called and prepared from the foundation of the world"?

Alma's teachings in Alma 13:3 refer specifically to priesthood holders. However, the principle he taught—that individuals received assignments and prepared to fulfill them "from the foundation of the world"—applies to all of us. President Spencer W. Kimball said: "In the world before we came here, faithful women were given certain assignments while faithful men were foreordained to certain priesthood tasks. While we do not now remember the particulars, this does not alter the glorious reality of what we once agreed to" (*Teachings of Presidents of the Church: Spencer W. Kimball* [2006], 215–16; see also D&C 138:55–56).

ALMA 14

Sometimes God allows the righteous to suffer.

Alma 14 tells of righteous people who suffered and even died because of their beliefs. You might wonder, as many do, why terrible things happen to people who are trying to live righteously. You may not find all the answers to this difficult question in Alma 14, but there is much to learn from the way Alma and Amulek responded to the situations they faced. What do their words and actions teach you about why the Lord sometimes allows righteous people to suffer? What do you learn from them about facing persecution?

See also Matthew 5:43–44; Mark 14:55–65; Romans 8:35–39; 1 Peter 4:12–14; Doctrine and Covenants 122:5–9.

Discipleship requires sacrifice.

It might be interesting to make a list of the things Amulek gave up to embrace the gospel (see Alma 10:4–5; 15:16) and compare it to a list of what he gained (see Alma 15:18; 16:13–15; 34:8). What are you willing to sacrifice in order to become a more faithful disciple?

Ideas for Family Scripture Study and Family Home Evening

As you read the scriptures with your family, the Spirit can help you know what principles to emphasize and discuss in order to meet the needs of your family. Here are some ideas.

Alma 13. Your family might benefit from noting every time the word "rest" appears in Alma 13. What other words and ideas appear with it? How does this help us understand what "the rest of the Lord" might mean? How is it different from physical rest?

Alma 13:10–12. To help your family visualize what these verses teach, maybe you could wash something together—like some white clothing. How do we feel when we are dirty? How do we feel when we become clean again? How are these feelings similar to what we feel when we sin and then repent and become clean through the Savior's Atonement?

Alma 15:1–12. What do we learn from Zeezrom's experience about the Lord's power to strengthen and heal us, even when we make mistakes? What role can the priesthood play in our receiving His strength and healing?

Alma 16:1–10. After reading these verses, you might read Alma 9:4. What do we learn by contrasting the way Zoram felt about the prophet's words with the way the people of Ammonihah felt? What are we doing to be faithful to the words of our living prophet?

For more ideas for teaching children, see this week's outline in *Come, Follow Me—For Primary.*

Improving Our Teaching

Be ready always. Teaching moments pass quickly, so take advantage of them when they arise. A tragedy in the world, for example, may be a chance to share principles from Alma 14 about why the Lord sometimes allows the innocent to suffer. (See *Teaching in the Savior's Way,* 16.)

Alma and Amulek in Prison, by Gary L. Kapp

Ammon and King Lamoni, by Scott M. Snow

Alma 17–22

"I WILL MAKE AN INSTRUMENT OF THEE"

As you read Alma 17–22, record impressions that come to you and act on them. Doing so will show the Lord your willingness to receive more personal revelation.

RECORD YOUR IMPRESSIONS

Think of all of the reasons people might give for not sharing the gospel: "I don't know enough" or "I'm not sure they would be interested" or maybe "What if I offend them?" Maybe you've found yourself thinking similar things at times. The Nephites had an additional reason for not sharing the gospel with the Lamanites: they were "a wild and a hardened and a ferocious people; a people who delighted in murdering the Nephites" (Alma 17:14; see also Alma 26:23–25). But the sons of Mosiah had an even stronger reason why they felt they *must* share the gospel with the Lamanites: "They were desirous that salvation should be declared to every creature, for they could not bear that any human soul should perish" (Mosiah 28:3). This love that inspired Ammon and his brothers can also inspire you to share the gospel with your family, friends, and acquaintances—even those who may not seem likely to accept it.

Ideas for Personal Scripture Study

ALMA 17:1–4

As I strengthen my own faith, I can more effectively share the gospel.

Have you ever been reunited with old friends and felt the way Alma did—overjoyed that they had stayed strong in the faith? (see Alma 17:1–2). What do you learn from the sons of Mosiah about how to keep your faith in the gospel and commitment to it strong? As you ponder the spiritual strength of the sons of Mosiah, what do you feel inspired to do?

How did the spiritual preparation of the sons of Mosiah affect their work with the Lamanites? Perhaps you could use this opportunity to evaluate your efforts to teach the gospel "with power and authority of God" (Alma 17:3).

ALMA 17:6–12

I can be an instrument in God's hands to bring salvation to His children.

President Thomas S. Monson said, "I always want the Lord to know that if He needs an errand run, Tom Monson will run that errand for Him" ("On the Lord's Errand: The Life of Thomas S. Monson," video, ChurchofJesusChrist.org). As you read Alma 17:6–12, look for what the sons of Mosiah did so they could be instruments in God's hands. How can you be an instrument in God's hands to bless others? What do you learn from their example that gives you courage to do what the Lord needs you to do?

See also Dallin H. Oaks, "Sharing the Restored Gospel," *Ensign* or *Liahona,* Nov. 2016, 57–60.

ALMA 17–18

I can help others prepare to receive the gospel.

Lamoni was the leader of "a wild and a hardened and a ferocious people" (Alma 17:14), yet he overcame years of tradition and accepted the gospel of Jesus Christ. As you read about Ammon's interactions with Lamoni, notice what Ammon did that might have helped Lamoni be more receptive to his message. If thoughts come to you about what you can do to share the gospel with others, write down these promptings.

It may also be helpful to mark or write down the truths that Ammon taught Lamoni (see Alma 18:24–39) and the truths that Aaron taught Lamoni's father (see Alma 22:1–16). What do these verses suggest to you about the truths you can share with others to help them seek a testimony of the gospel?

Minerva K. Teichert (1888–1976), *Ammon Saves the King's Flocks,* 1935–1945, oil on masonite, 35 x 48 inches. Brigham Young University Museum of Art.

ALMA 18–22

My testimony can have a far-reaching influence.

Though the accounts of conversion we read about in the scriptures often involve dramatic events, at their core we usually find individuals who had the courage to speak up and share their witness with others. One way to study the events in Alma 18–22 is to look for the far-reaching effects of one person bearing his or her testimony. Maybe you could record what you find in a diagram like this one:

Ammon shared the gospel with _____, who shared the gospel with _____, and the result was _____.

ALMA 19:36

The Lord's arm is extended to me when I repent.

At the conclusion of the account of Lamoni's conversion, Mormon taught something important about the Lord's character. What does Alma 19:36 suggest to you about the Lord's character? When have you felt the Lord's arm extended toward you? How can you help those you love feel His mercy?

Ideas for Family Scripture Study and Family Home Evening

As you read the scriptures with your family, the Spirit can help you know what principles to emphasize and discuss in order to meet the needs of your family. Here are some ideas.

Alma 17–19. How can you make the accounts in these chapters come to life for your family? You could act out the story of Ammon protecting the sheep or the story of Abish gathering the multitude to witness the power of God. Perhaps family members could draw pictures of different parts of the story and use the pictures to tell the story. What will your family do to follow the examples of Ammon and Abish?

Alma 18:24–39. Perhaps your family members could read Alma 18:24–39 together and identify the truths that Ammon taught Lamoni. Why do we think that

Ammon taught Lamoni these truths first? Why is it important for us to have a testimony of these truths?

Alma 20:8–15. What can we learn from how Lamoni responded to his father? How can we follow Lamoni's example in standing up for what is right? (For some examples, see the video "Dare to Stand Alone" on ChurchofJesusChrist.org.)

Alma 22:15–18. Review Alma 20:23 to see what Lamoni's father was willing to give up in order to save his life. Then review Alma 22:15 to see what he was willing to give up in order to receive the joy of the gospel. What was he willing to give up in order to know God? (see verse 18). Perhaps family members could each write a plan to give up something in order to know God more fully.

For more ideas for teaching children, see this week's outline in *Come, Follow Me—For Primary.*

Improving Personal Study

Identify and apply principles. Though the details of scripture stories may not seem to apply to you, the principles in these accounts often do. As you read about Ammon and Aaron, what principles about sharing the gospel do you find?

The wife of King Lamoni rose from the ground, praising Jesus. *Oh, Blessed Jesus,* by Walter Rane

Anti-Nephi-Lehies Bury Their Weapons of War, by Jody Livingston

Alma 23–29

THEY "NEVER DID FALL AWAY"

As you study Alma 23–29, what messages do you find for yourself and your family? What can you share in your Church classes?

RECORD YOUR IMPRESSIONS _____

_____

_____

Do you sometimes wonder whether people can really change? Maybe you worry about whether you can overcome poor choices you've made or bad habits you've developed, or you may have similar worries about loved ones. If so, the story of the Anti-Nephi-Lehies can help you. These people were the sworn enemies of the Nephites. When Ammon and his brethren decided to preach the gospel to them, the Nephites "laughed [them] to scorn." Killing the Lamanites seemed like a more plausible solution than converting them. (See Alma 26:23–25.)

But the Lamanites did change—through the converting power of the Lord. Where once they were known as "a hardened and a ferocious people" (Alma 17:14), they became "distinguished for their zeal towards God" (Alma 27:27). In fact, they "never did fall away" (Alma 23:6).

Maybe you have false traditions to abandon or "weapons of . . . rebellion" to lay down (Alma 23:7). Or maybe you just need to be a little more zealous in your testimony and a little less prone to falling away. No matter what changes you need, Alma 23–29 can give you hope that, through the atoning power of Jesus Christ, long-lasting change is possible.

Ideas for Personal Scripture Study

ALMA 23:1–5

When God's children accept the gospel, great blessings follow.

When the king of the Lamanites declared that the word of God should "have no obstruction" among his people (see Alma 23:1–5), he opened the door to great blessings for them. As you read Alma 23–29, look for these blessings. How can you ensure that the word of God has "no obstruction" in your life or in your family?

ALMA 23–25; 27

My conversion to Jesus Christ and His gospel changes my life.

The Lamanites who were visited by Ammon and his brethren seemed to be unlikely candidates for conversion—they were trapped by the traditions of their fathers and their own wickedness. Yet many of them accepted the gospel of Jesus Christ and made fundamental changes in their lives. As a symbol of their own conversion, these Lamanites called themselves Anti-Nephi-Lehies. (The meaning of "anti" in this case is not the same as "anti" in "anti-Christ.")

Reflecting on the conversion of these Lamanites might prompt you to ponder your own conversion "unto the Lord" (Alma 23:6). One way to study these chapters could be to identify how the conversion of the Anti-Nephi-Lehies changed their lives. The following verses can get you started.

As you ponder the changes in the Anti-Nephi-Lehies, consider how your own conversion to Christ is changing you. What do you feel you still need to change so that the gospel can have greater power in your life?

Alma 23:6–7_____

Alma 23:17–18_____

Alma 24:11–19_____

Alma 25:13–16_____

Alma 27:26–30_____

ALMA 24:7–19; 26:17–22

God is merciful.

While the sins that Ammon and the Anti-Nephi-Lehies had to overcome were likely quite different from anything in your life, we all rely on the mercy of God. What do you find in Alma 24:7–19 and 26:17–22 that helps you understand His mercy? As you read, you might think about these things: the ways you have been invited to repent, your experiences with repentance, how you have tried to avoid sinning again, and the blessings that have come to you through repentance. When you read the verses in this way, what do you learn about God's mercy in your life?

ALMA 26; 29

Serving the Lord brings joy.

Despite their different experiences, Ammon and Alma expressed similar feelings about their missionary labors. Consider reading Alma 26 and 29 and comparing them. What similarities do you notice? What words and phrases are repeated? What can you learn from Ammon and Alma about how to find true joy in spite of your challenges? (To review the challenges Alma faced, see the chapter headings for Alma 5–16. To review the challenges of Ammon and his brethren, see the chapter headings for Alma 17–28.)

ALMA 26:5–7

What are sheaves and garners?

At harvest time, grain is often gathered into bundles called *sheaves* and placed in storehouses, sometimes called *garners.* Elder David A. Bednar shared a possible interpretation of the symbolism in Alma 26:5: "The sheaves in this analogy represent newly baptized members of the Church. The garners are the holy temples" ("Honorably Hold a Name and Standing," *Ensign* or *Liahona,* May 2009, 97). Consider what the analogy in Alma 26:5–7 teaches you about the importance of temple covenants.

Ideas for Family Scripture Study and Family Home Evening

As you read the scriptures with your family, the Spirit can help you know what principles to emphasize and discuss in order to meet the needs of your family. Here are some ideas.

Alma 24:6–19. Why did the Anti-Nephi-Lehies bury their weapons "deep in the earth"? (Alma 24:16). Maybe family members would enjoy writing on pieces of paper things they would like to overcome or abandon. They could then dig a hole and bury the papers.

Alma 24:7–12. Studying these verses can help your family understand the wonderful gift of repentance. What did the Anti-Nephi-Lehies do to repent of their sins? How did the Lord help them repent? What can we learn from this example?

Alma 24:20–27. What have we seen that testifies of the truth of Mormon's declaration: "Thus we see that the Lord worketh in many ways to the salvation of his people"? (Alma 24:27).

Alma 26:2. How would your family answer Ammon's questions in Alma 26:2? Perhaps you could make a list of their answers on a large piece of paper and hang it in a place where everyone can see it. Encourage family members to add to it as they think of other blessings God has "bestowed upon us."

Alma 29:9. How were Ammon and Alma instruments in God's hands? Consider looking at tools or instruments in your home and discussing how they are each helpful to your family. How does this help us understand how we can each be "an instrument in the hands of God"?

For more ideas for teaching children, see this week's outline in *Come, Follow Me—For Primary.*

Improving Our Teaching

Use variety. Varying your approach to family scripture study can help family members stay interested and involved. For example, after a family member reads a verse, he or she could ask other family members to restate in their own words what was just read.

Illustration of the Anti-Nephi-Lehies burying their weapons, by Dan Burr

All Things Denote There Is a God (Alma and Korihor), by Walter Rane

Alma 30–31

"THE VIRTUE OF THE WORD OF GOD"

Alma testified of the "powerful effect" of the word of God (Alma 31:5). As you read Alma 30–31, record your impressions as you feel the powerful effect God's word has on you.

RECORD YOUR IMPRESSIONS

The accounts in Alma 30–31 clearly demonstrate the power of words—for evil and for good. The "flattering" and "great swelling words" of a false teacher named Korihor threatened to bring "many souls down to destruction" (Alma 30:31, 47). Similarly, the teachings of a Nephite dissenter named Zoram led a whole group of people to fall "into great errors" and "pervert the ways of the Lord" (Alma 31:9, 11).

In contrast, Alma had unwavering faith that the word of God would have a "more powerful effect upon the minds of the people than the sword, or anything else" (Alma 31:5)—including the words of Korihor and Zoram. Alma's words expressed eternal truth and drew upon the powers of heaven to silence Korihor (see Alma 30:39–50), and they invited heaven's blessing on those who went with him to bring the Zoramites back to the truth (see Alma 31:31–38). These are valuable examples for followers of Christ today, when "great swelling words" and "great errors" again have a powerful effect on the minds of the people (Alma 30:31; 31:9). But we can find truth by trusting, as Alma did, "the virtue of the word of God" (Alma 31:5).

Ideas for Personal Scripture Study

ALMA 30:6, 12

What is an anti-Christ?

In Alma 30, Korihor is called "Anti-Christ" (verse 6). An anti-Christ is "one who would assume the guise of Christ but in reality would be opposed to Christ (1 John 2:18–22; 4:3–6; 2 John 1:7). In a broader sense it is anyone or anything that counterfeits the true gospel or plan of salvation and that openly or secretly is set up in opposition to Christ" (Bible Dictionary, "Antichrist").

What "counterfeits [of] the true gospel" do you notice in today's world? For example, Sister Julie B. Beck, former Relief Society General President, taught, "Any doctrine or principle [we] hear from the world that is antifamily is also anti-Christ" ("Teaching the Doctrine of the Family," *Ensign,* Mar. 2011, 15).

Korihor Confronts Alma, by Robert T. Barrett

ALMA 30:6–60

The Book of Mormon can help me resist the influence of those who try to deceive me.

As you read Alma 30:6–31, the teachings of Korihor may sound familiar. That's because, as President Ezra Taft Benson taught, the Book of Mormon reveals and can fortify us against "the evil designs, strategies, and

doctrines of the devil in our day. The type of apostates in the Book of Mormon are similar to the type we have today. God, with his infinite foreknowledge, so molded the Book of Mormon that we might see the error and know how to combat false educational, political, religious, and philosophical concepts of our time" (*Teachings of Presidents of the Church: Ezra Taft Benson,* [2014], 132).

Consider making a list of the false doctrines Korihor taught in Alma 30:6–31. What are some of the consequences of believing these teachings? For instance, what is the result of believing that "when a man [is] dead, that [is] the end thereof"? (Alma 30:18). What false doctrines taught by Korihor are similar to false doctrines you've noticed in the world today?

Reading about the interaction between Korihor and Alma can help you prepare for situations when others may try to deceive you. It might help to study Alma 30:29–60 to understand how Korihor was deceived (see especially verses 52–53). What can you learn from Alma's response to Korihor's teachings? (see Alma 30:31–35).

ALMA 31

God's word has the power to lead people to righteousness.

The problem of the Zoramites separating from the Nephites may have seemed to some like it needed a political or military solution (see Alma 31:1–4). But Alma had learned to trust "the virtue of the word of God" (Alma 31:5). What do you learn from Alma 31:5 about the power of God's word? How have you seen the word of God lead "people to do that which [is] just"? (Alma 31:5). Ponder how you can "try" (use or test) the word of God to help someone you love.

To further understand Alma's approach to rescuing others, you could compare his attitudes, feelings, and actions with those of the Zoramites, as described in Alma 31. A table like the following one might help. What differences do you notice? How do you feel you could be more like Alma?

Zoramites	Alma
Believed those outside their group were condemned to hell (Alma 31:17).	Believed the Zoramites were his "brethren" and their souls were "precious" (Alma 31:35).
Set their hearts on riches (Alma 31:24, 28).	Desired to bring souls to Jesus Christ (Alma 31:34).

Ideas for Family Scripture Study and Family Home Evening

As you read the scriptures with your family, the Spirit can help you know what principles to emphasize and discuss in order to meet the needs of your family. Here are some ideas.

Alma 30:44. Consider reading and discussing Alma 30:44 together as you go on a walk outside or look at pictures of God's creations. Family members could share what they see that testifies of God. How do these things—or other experiences we've had—help us know God is real?

Alma 30:56–60. What do we learn from Alma 30:56–60 about how the devil treats his followers? What can we do to protect our home against his influence?

Alma 31:20–38. After reading Alma 31:20–38 with your family, you could discuss the following questions: How was Alma's prayer different from the prayer of the Zoramites? How can we follow Alma's example in our personal and family prayers?

Younger children could put a rock under their pillows to help them remember to pray every morning and night. They also might enjoy decorating their rock.

Alma 31:23. What are we doing each day in our home to learn about and speak of God?

For more ideas for teaching children, see this week's outline in *Come, Follow Me—For Primary*.

Improving Personal Study

Prepare your surroundings. "Our surroundings can profoundly affect our ability to learn and feel truth" (*Teaching in the Savior's Way*, 15). Try to find a place to study the scriptures that will invite the influence of the Holy Ghost. Uplifting music and pictures can also invite the Spirit.

The Rameumptom, by Del Parson

Alma 32–35

"PLANT THIS WORD IN YOUR HEARTS"

Record the spiritual impressions you receive as you study Alma 32–35. What do you feel inspired to do because of what you learn?

RECORD YOUR IMPRESSIONS

For the Zoramites, prayer was a self-centered, routine practice that happened only once a week. It consisted of standing where all could see and repeating vain, self-satisfied words. Perhaps worse, the Zoramites lacked faith in Jesus Christ—even denied His existence—and persecuted the poor (see Alma 31:9–25). By contrast, Alma and Amulek boldly taught that prayer has more to do with what happens in our hearts than on a public platform. And if it doesn't lead to compassion toward those in need, it is "vain, and availeth . . . nothing" (Alma

34:28). Most important, it is an expression of faith in Jesus Christ, who offers redemption through His "infinite and eternal sacrifice" (Alma 34:10). Such faith, Alma explained, is born of humility and a "desire to believe" (Alma 32:27). It grows gradually, like a tree, and requires constant nourishment. As you read Alma 32–35, you might consider your own faith and prayers; do you ever feel any Zoramite-like attitudes creeping in? How will you nourish your faith in Jesus Christ so it will become "a tree springing up unto everlasting life"? (Alma 32:41).

Ideas for Personal Scripture Study

ALMA 32:1–16

I can choose to be humble.

Alma perceived that the poor Zoramites were humble and "in a preparation to hear the word" (Alma 32:6). As you read Alma 32:1–16, think about how you prepare to hear the word of God.

What experiences have humbled you? What have you done to become more humble? These verses could teach you how to choose humility rather than be compelled to be humble. For example, what is the difference between being "poor as to things of the world" and being "poor in heart"? (verse 3). What does it mean to "humble [yourself] because of the word"? (verse 14).

See also "Humility," Gospel Topics, topics.ChurchofJesusChrist.org.

ALMA 32:17–43; 33–34

I exercise faith in Jesus Christ by planting and nourishing His word in my heart.

Why do you think Alma spoke about planting a seed in response to the Zoramites' questions about worship? What is the seed that Alma spoke of? (see Alma 32:28; 33:22–23). As you read Alma 32:17–43, note words and phrases that help you understand how to exercise faith in Jesus Christ and His word. What do you learn about what faith is and what it is not? Then, as you read chapters 33–34, search for answers to the Zoramites' question "How [do we] plant the seed?" (Alma 33:1).

Here's another way to study Alma 32–34: Draw pictures representing different phases of a seed's growth. Then label each picture with words from Alma 32:28–43 that help you understand how to plant and nourish the word in your heart.

See also Matthew 13:3–8, 18–23; Hebrews 11; Neil L. Andersen, "Faith Is Not by Chance, but by Choice," *Ensign* or *Liahona,* Nov. 2015, 65–68; "Faith in Jesus Christ," Gospel Topics, topics.ChurchofJesusChrist.org.

ALMA 33:2–11; 34:17–29

I can worship God in prayer, anytime and anywhere.

Alma and Amulek's counsel about worship and prayer was meant to correct specific misunderstandings the Zoramites had (see Alma 31:13–23). But the truths they taught can help any us of understand prayer and worship better. Maybe you could make a list of truths about prayer that you find in Alma 33:2–11 and 34:17–29. Next to that list, make a list of possible misconceptions about prayer that these truths correct (see Alma 31:12–23). How will the things you learn from these verses affect the way you pray and worship?

ALMA 33:3–17

Who were Zenos and Zenock?

Zenos and Zenock were prophets who testified of Jesus Christ during Old Testament times, but their teachings are not found in the Old Testament. The Nephites had access to the teachings of these prophets, probably because they were included in the brass plates that Nephi obtained from Laban. They are also mentioned in 1 Nephi 19:10–12; Jacob 5:1; and Helaman 8:19–20.

ALMA 34:30–41

"This life is the time . . . to prepare to meet God."

As you read Alma 34:30–41, consider how you might "improve [your] time while in this life" (verse 33). How can repentance and patience help you prepare to meet God? Are there changes you need to make that you have been procrastinating? Be sure to act on any spiritual impressions you receive.

See also Alma 12:24; Larry R. Lawrence, "What Lack I Yet?" *Ensign* or *Liahona,* Nov. 2015, 33–35.

Ideas for Family Scripture Study and Family Home Evening

As you read the scriptures with your family, the Spirit can help you know what principles to emphasize and discuss in order to meet the needs of your family. Here are some ideas.

Alma 32:9–11; 33:2–11; 34:38–39. What would it be like if we were allowed to worship and pray only on Sunday? As you read these verses together, family members could discuss how they can worship every day and why they are thankful that they can.

Alma 32:28–43. A picture of a tree accompanies this outline; you might use it to illustrate Alma's words in these verses. Or your family could go for a walk to find plants at different stages of growth and read verses from Alma 32 that compare a growing plant to our faith. Maybe each family member could plant a seed and discuss what we need to do to help it grow. Over the coming weeks you could check on your seeds and remind each other of the need to continually nourish our testimonies.

Alma 33:2–11; 34:17–29. What do these verses suggest about how we can improve our individual and family prayers?

Alma 34:31. What experiences have shown us that when we repent, we begin "immediately" to experience the blessings of the plan of redemption?

Alma 34:33–35. Does your family know what it means to procrastinate? Maybe someone can share examples of procrastination and its negative consequences. What does it mean to "procrastinate the day of [our] repentance"?

For more ideas for teaching children, see this week's outline in *Come, Follow Me—For Primary.*

Improving Our Teaching

Draw pictures. You might let family members draw as they learn from the scriptures. For instance, they might enjoy drawing a seed growing into a tree as they study Alma 32.

"Because of your diligence and your faith and your patience with the word in nourishing it, . . . behold, by and by ye shall pluck the fruit thereof, which is most precious" (Alma 32:42).

Illustration of a man praying by Joshua Dennis

Alma 36–38

"LOOK TO GOD AND LIVE"

"As you feel the joy that comes from understanding the gospel, you will want to apply what you learn" (*Preach My Gospel* [2004], 19). Record your thoughts and impressions about how to apply the truths you are learning.

RECORD YOUR IMPRESSIONS⎯⎯

⎯⎯

⎯⎯

When Alma saw wickedness around him, he felt deep "sorrow," "tribulation," and "anguish of soul" (Alma 8:14). "Wickedness among this people," he said of the Zoramites, "doth pain my soul" (Alma 31:30). He felt something similar after returning from his mission to the Zoramites—he observed that "the hearts of the people began to wax hard, and that they began to be offended because of the strictness of the word," and this made his heart "exceedingly sorrowful" (Alma 35:15). What did Alma do about what he saw and felt? He didn't simply become discouraged or cynical about the state of the world. Instead, "he caused that his sons should be gathered together" and taught them "things pertaining unto righteousness" (Alma 35:16). He taught them that "there is no other way or means whereby man can be saved, only in and through Christ. . . . Behold, he is the word of truth and righteousness" (Alma 38:9).

Ideas for Personal Scripture Study

I can be born of God as I am humble and repent.

Few will have experiences as dramatic as Alma's conversion. But there are principles in his experience that we can all learn from and apply, because everyone must be "born of God" (Alma 36:23). As you read Alma 36, look for principles you can apply. For instance, how does someone who has been born of God feel about sin? about Jesus Christ? You could also look for changes you might expect to see in the beliefs and actions of someone who is born of God.

See also Mosiah 5:7; 27:25–26; Alma 5:14; 22:15; Helaman 3:35; "Conversion," Gospel Topics, topics.ChurchofJesusChrist.org.

Jesus Christ atoned for the sins of the world.

You may notice some repetition in Alma's account of his conversion in this chapter. That's because Alma 36 is a great example of a form of Hebrew poetry called chiasmus, in which words or ideas are presented in a certain order, leading to a central idea, and then repeated in reverse order. In Alma 36, the idea in verse 3 is repeated in verse 27, the idea in verse 5 is repeated in verse 26, and so on. The central idea is the most important message of the chiasmus. See if you can find the central idea in verses 17–18. Notice how catching "hold upon this thought" affected Alma and changed his life. How has this truth affected you? What other repeated ideas do you find in this passage?

How does this account of repentance and forgiveness inspire you to follow Alma's example and turn to the Savior?

For more information about chiasmus, see *Book of Mormon Student Manual* (Church Educational System manual [2009], 232–33).

The scriptures have been preserved "for a wise purpose."

Have you ever thought about what a miracle and blessing it is to have the scriptures today? God has "entrusted [us] with these things, which are sacred" (Alma 37:14). As you read Alma 37, look for the blessings that come from having the scriptures. How have you experienced these blessings? How can we use the scriptures to help "show forth [God's] power unto future generations"? (Alma 37:18).

In Alma 37:38–47, Alma compares "the word of Christ" to the Liahona. As you ponder this comparison, reflect on the ways you have experienced the miracle and power of Christ's teachings "day by day" (Alma 37:40).

See also D. Todd Christofferson, "The Blessing of Scripture," *Ensign* or *Liahona,* May 2010, 32–35.

The scriptures teach us how to follow God.

"By small and simple things are great things brought to pass."

Sometimes we may feel like our problems are so big and complicated that the solutions must be big and complicated too. Yet time and time again, the Lord chooses to use "small and simple things" (Alma 37:6) to accomplish His work and bless the lives of His children. As you read Alma 37:6–7, ponder and record ways you've seen this principle at work in your life. What are some small and simple things the Lord uses to bless you and accomplish His work?

See also Alma 37:41–46; Dallin H. Oaks, "Small and Simple Things," *Ensign* or *Liahona,* May 2018, 89–92.

Ideas for Family Scripture Study and Family Home Evening

As you read the scriptures with your family, the Spirit can help you know what principles to emphasize and discuss in order to meet the needs of your family. Here are some ideas.

Alma 36:5–26. Although Alma's experience was extraordinary, his conversion illustrates several principles that apply to all of us. Invite each family member to select a verse from Alma 36:5–26 that teaches about being "born of God." What do we learn from these verses? Perhaps family members could share how they have applied the principles Alma described.

Alma 36:18–21, 24. How could we use these verses to help someone see that repentance is a joyful experience, not a dreadful one? How can repentance inspire us to share the gospel with others?

Alma 37:6–7, 38–46. What are some of the "small and simple things" (Alma 37:6) that bring about great things in our lives? In what ways is the word of Christ like the Liahona? How can we help each other study the scriptures more diligently?

Alma 37:35. Why is it wise to learn to keep the commandments while "in [our] youth"?

Alma 38:12. Does your family know what a bridle is? Maybe you could show them a picture of one and talk about how it is used to control an animal. What does it mean to "bridle [our] passions"? How does bridling our passions help us be "filled with love"?

For more ideas for teaching children, see this week's outline in *Come, Follow Me—For Primary.*

Improving Personal Study

Record impressions. When you record spiritual impressions, you show the Lord that you value His direction, and He will bless you with more frequent revelation. As you study, write down your thoughts. (See *Teaching in the Savior's Way,* 12, 30.)

Angel Appears to Alma and the Sons of Mosiah, by Clark Kelley Price

Woman, Why Weepest Thou? by Mark R. Pugh

Alma 39–42

"THE GREAT PLAN OF HAPPINESS"

As you study Alma 39–42, the Holy Ghost can give you insights about things that are happening in your life.

RECORD YOUR IMPRESSIONS _____

_____

_____

When someone we love has made a serious mistake, it can be hard to know how to respond. Part of what makes Alma 39–42 so valuable is that it reveals how Alma—a disciple of Christ who once had his own grievous sins to repent of—handled such a situation. Alma's son Corianton had committed sexual sin, and Alma, as he often did, trusted the power of true doctrine to encourage repentance (see Alma 4:19; 31:5). In these chapters, we observe Alma's boldness in condemning sin and his tenderness and love for Corianton. And ultimately, we sense Alma's confidence that the Savior "shall come to take away [sins and] declare glad tidings of salvation" to those who repent (Alma 39:15). The fact that Corianton eventually returned to the work of the ministry (see Alma 49:30) can give us hope for forgiveness and redemption when we are "trouble[d]" (Alma 42:29) about our own sins or the sins of someone we love.

Ideas for Personal Scripture Study

Sexual sin is an abomination in the sight of the Lord.

To impress upon his son the seriousness of sexual sin, Alma taught "that these things are an abomination in the sight of the Lord" (Alma 39:5). Why is chastity important to you? Why is it important to the Lord? The following explanation from Elder Jeffrey R. Holland may be helpful:

"Clearly among His greatest concerns regarding mortality are how one gets into this world and how one gets out of it. He has set very strict limits in these matters.

". . . Human intimacy is reserved for a married couple because it is the ultimate symbol of total union, a totality and a union ordained and defined by God. . . . Marriage was intended to mean the complete merger of a man and a woman. . . . This is a union of such completeness that we use the word *seal* to convey its eternal promise" ("Personal Purity," *Ensign,* Nov. 1998, 76).

Consider the counsel Alma gave Corianton in Alma 39:8–15. How does it help you further understand the importance of the law of chastity and how to overcome temptation? Alma's teachings also demonstrate how eager the Lord is to forgive us when we repent and that there is hope for all of us. As you read Alma 39–42 this week, look for evidence of God's mercy. How has God's mercy blessed you?

See also "Sexual Purity," *For the Strength of Youth,* 35–37.

I will be resurrected and stand before God to be judged.

When Alma noticed that Corianton had questions about the Resurrection, he taught him about what happens after we die. What truths did Alma teach in chapters 40–41 that would have been helpful for Corianton—and anybody who has sinned—to understand? You might organize what you learn by identifying the topics that Alma addresses (such as the spirit world, resurrection, and restoration) and then writing down what Alma teaches about each one. How can remembering these truths help you when you feel tempted or are seeking forgiveness?

I can seek answers to my gospel questions in faith.

Sometimes we might think that prophets know the answer to every gospel question. But notice that throughout chapter 40, Alma had several unanswered questions about life after death. What did he do to find answers? What did he do when he didn't have answers? Consider how Alma's example might help you with gospel questions you have.

Prayer is one way we can find answers to gospel questions.

ALMA 42

The Atonement of Jesus Christ makes the plan of redemption possible.

Corianton believed that punishment for sins was not fair (see Alma 42:1). But Alma taught that there is a way to escape from the "state of misery" that sin puts us in: repentance and faith in the Atonement of Jesus Christ, which is both merciful and just (see Alma 42:15). As you read Alma 42, look for how the Savior's Atonement makes it possible for you to receive mercy without "rob[bing] justice" (verse 25). What truths do you find in this chapter that help you feel His mercy?

Ideas for Family Scripture Study and Family Home Evening

As you read the scriptures with your family, the Spirit can help you know what principles to emphasize and discuss in order to meet the needs of your family. Here are some ideas.

Alma 39:1–9. Would your family benefit from a discussion about the law of chastity? If so, consider using the following resources according to your family's needs: Alma 39:1–9; "Sexual Purity," *For the Strength of Youth*, 35–37; "Chastity," Gospel Topics, topics.ChurchofJesusChrist.org; overcomingpornography.org; and the videos "What Should I Do When I See Pornography?" and "I Choose to Be Pure" (ChurchofJesusChrist.org). Ponder how you can help your family understand

the blessings of chastity and of intimacy in marriage (for example, see the video "How to Talk to Your Kids about Intimacy" on ChurchofJesusChrist.org).

Alma 39:9–15. What do we learn from these verses about how to avoid sin?

Alma 42:4. You could play a game in which pieces of paper with Christlike attributes or gospel principles written on them are scattered around the room. You could see how many pieces of paper family members can gather in a certain amount of time, then discuss how the things written on the papers can help us become more like God. How is the "time granted" to us on earth like the time allotted in this game? How can we use our "probationary time" on earth to become more like the Savior?

Alma 42:12–15, 22–24. Perhaps you could illustrate the relationship between justice and mercy by using a drawing of a simple scale to discuss questions like these: What happens to the scale when we sin? What does justice require for the scale to be balanced? How does the Savior meet the demands of justice and make mercy possible?

For more ideas for teaching children, see this week's outline in *Come, Follow Me—For Primary*.

Improving Our Teaching

Focus on principles that will bless your family. As you prayerfully study the word of God, ask yourself, "What do I find here that will be especially meaningful to my family?" Seek the direction of the Spirit as you ponder how to help your family discover these truths.

This My Son, by Elspeth Caitlin Young

For the Blessings of Liberty, by Scott M. Snow

Alma 43–52

"STAND FAST IN THE FAITH OF CHRIST"

It may seem that the events described in Alma 43–52 are not particularly relevant to you. But as in all scripture, the Lord has a message for you. Prayerfully seek it.

RECORD YOUR IMPRESSIONS _____

_____

_____

When we read these words at the beginning of Alma chapter 43—"And now I return to an account of the wars between the Nephites and the Lamanites"—it's natural to wonder why Mormon included these war stories when he had limited space on the plates (see Words of Mormon 1:5). It's true that we have our share of wars in the latter days, but there is value in his words beyond the descriptions of the strategy and tragedy of war. His words also prepare us for the war in which "we are all enlisted" (*Hymns,* no. 250), the war we are fighting each day against the forces of evil. This war is very real, and the outcome affects our eternal lives. Like the Nephites, we are "inspired by a better cause," which is "our God, our religion, and freedom, and our peace, our [families]." Moroni called this "the cause of the Christians," the same cause we are fighting for today (Alma 43:45; 46:12, 16).

Ideas for Personal Scripture Study

ALMA 43–52

The battles in the Book of Mormon teach me about my battles against evil.

Reading about the wars between the Nephites and Lamanites might be more meaningful to you if you look for parallels to your personal spiritual battles. As you read Alma 43–52, notice what the Nephites did that made them successful (or unsuccessful). Then ponder how you can use what you learn to help you win your spiritual battles. As you study verses like the following, write your thoughts about how you can follow the Nephites' example:

Alma 43:19 *The Nephites were prepared with armor. (I can strive to prepare myself with spiritual armor.)*

Alma 43:23–24 *They sought the prophet's guidance.*

Alma 44:1–4_____

Alma 45:1_____

Alma 46:11–20_____

Alma 48:7–9_____

Alma 49:3, 12–14_____

Also notice how the Lamanites and the Nephite dissenters tried to defeat the Nephites. These things can warn you about how the adversary might try to attack you. As you study, write how Satan might attack you in similar ways:

Alma 43:8 *Zerahemnah sought to make his people angry so he would have power over them. (When I become angry with other people, I give Satan power over me.)*

Alma 43:29 *The Lamanites wanted to bring the Nephites into bondage.*

Alma 46:10_____

Alma 47:10–19_____

Minerva K. Teichert (1888–1976), *Defense of a Nephite City,* 1935, oil on masonite, 36 x 48 inches. Brigham Young University Museum of Art.

ALMA 46:11–28; 48:7–17

As I strive to be faithful like Moroni, I will become more like the Savior.

Do you wish you could become more like the Savior and lessen the power of the adversary in your life? One way is to follow the admonition in Alma 48:17 to become "like unto Moroni." Pay attention to Moroni's attributes and actions that are described throughout Alma 43–52 but particularly in 46:11–28 and 48:7–17. What impresses you about this "mighty man"? How can attributes and actions like his weaken the power of the devil in your life? Ponder what you feel inspired to do to follow Moroni's example and become more like the Savior.

ALMA 47

Satan tempts and deceives us little by little.

Satan knows that most of us aren't willing to commit big sins or believe big lies. Therefore, he uses subtle lies and temptations to lead us into seemingly small sins—as many as he thinks we will accept. He continues to do this until we have strayed far from the safety of righteous living.

You can find this pattern in the account of Amalickiah deceiving Lehonti, found in Alma 47. As you study, ponder how Satan may be trying to deceive you, as described by Elder Robert D. Hales:

"The traitorous Amalickiah urged Lehonti to 'come down' and meet him in the valley. But when Lehonti left the high ground, he was poisoned 'by degrees' until he died, and his army fell into Amalickiah's hands (see Alma 47). By arguments and accusations, some people bait us to leave the high ground. The high ground is where the light is. . . . It is the safe ground" ("Christian Courage: The Price of Discipleship," *Ensign* or *Liahona,* Nov. 2008, 74).

See also 2 Nephi 26:22; 28:21–22.

ALMA 50–51

Unity brings safety.

In the circumstances recorded at the beginning of Alma 50, it looked like the Lamanites had no chance against the Nephites. The armor, fortifications, and unified efforts of the Nephites made them seem unconquerable (see Alma 49:28–30 and 50:17–20). But the Lamanites soon captured many of their cities—including those that Moroni had fortified (see Alma 51:26–27). How did that happen? Look for answers as you read these chapters (see particularly Alma 51:1–12). Ponder what warnings this account may have for you and your family.

Ideas for Family Scripture Study and Family Home Evening

As you read the scriptures with your family, the Spirit can help you know what principles to emphasize and discuss in order to meet the needs of your family. Here are some ideas.

Alma 45:2–8. Reading these verses together might inspire your family to hold one-on-one gospel conversations with family members, as Alma did with Helaman.

Alma 46:12–22. The title of liberty inspired the Nephites to keep the commandments of God and defend their faith. What inspires us to do the same? Perhaps your family could create your own title of liberty—a flag or banner with words or images that remind you to keep the commandments of God each day.

Alma 48:7–9; 49:1–9; 50:1–6. As your family reads about the Nephites' fortifications, you could discuss how you are fortifying your home against the adversary. Children might enjoy building a fort out of objects like chairs and blankets, or they could draw what they imagine the Nephite fortifications looked like.

Alma 51:1–12. What do these verses teach about what can happen within our family when we have contention? How can we increase our unity?

For more ideas for teaching children, see this week's outline in *Come, Follow Me—For Primary.*

Improving Personal Study

Ask questions as you study. As you study the scriptures, ask yourself questions that can help you ponder how well you are living by what you read.

Title of Liberty, by Larry Conrad Winborg

Two Thousand Young Warriors, by Arnold Friberg

Alma 53–63

"PRESERVED BY HIS MARVELOUS POWER"

The accounts in Alma 53–63 can help you see the consequences of living gospel truths or rejecting them. As you read Alma 53–63, record promptings and ponder ways you can live the truths you learn.

RECORD YOUR IMPRESSIONS

When compared with the Lamanite armies, Helaman's "little army" (Alma 56:33) of 2,000 young Nephites shouldn't have stood a chance. Besides being few in number, Helaman's soldiers "were all . . . very young," and "they never had fought" (Alma 56:46–47). In some ways, their situation might seem familiar to those of us who sometimes feel outnumbered and overwhelmed in our latter-day battle against Satan and the forces of evil in the world.

But the army of Helaman had some advantages over the Lamanites that had nothing to do with numbers or military skill. They chose Helaman, a prophet, to lead them (Alma 53:19); "they had been taught by their mothers, that if they did not doubt, God would deliver them" (Alma 56:47); and they had "exceeding faith in that which they had been taught." As a result, they were protected by "the miraculous power of God" (Alma 57:26). Even though they were all wounded in battle, "there was not one soul of them who did perish" (Alma 57:25). So when life inflicts spiritual wounds on each of us, we can take courage—the message of Helaman's army is that "there [is] a just God, and whosoever [does] not doubt, [will] be preserved by his marvelous power" (Alma 57:26).

Ideas for Personal Scripture Study

ALMA 53:10–22; 56:43–48, 55–56; 57:20–27; 58:39–40

As I exercise faith in God, He will bless me by His marvelous power.

Miraculous stories like the victories of Helaman's young warriors may be hard to relate to because they seem so improbable. But one reason such stories are in the scriptures is to show us that when we have faith, God can work miracles in our lives. As you read about the stripling warriors in the following verses, look for clues about how they exercised their faith in God, what made their faith so strong, and what made the miracles possible: Alma 53:10–22; 56:43–48, 55–56; 57:20–27; and 58:39–40. The following table suggests one way you could record what you find.

Characteristics of Helaman's warriors:	
What they were taught:	
What they did:	
Blessings they received:	

After studying these verses, what do you feel inspired to do to exercise your faith?

Helaman mentioned the role of mothers in strengthening the faith of the stripling warriors (see Alma 56:47–48; 57:20–27). What roles have family members and others played in building your faith? What can you do to strengthen the faith of your family and friends?

They Did Not Doubt, by Joseph Brickey

ALMA 58:1–12, 31–37; 61

I can choose to think the best of others and not be offended.

Both Helaman and Pahoran had good reasons to be offended. Helaman was not receiving sufficient support for his armies, and Pahoran was falsely accused by Moroni of withholding that support (see Alma 58:4–9, 31–32; 60). What impresses you about their reactions in Alma 58:1–12, 31–37 and Alma 61? How can you follow their example in similar situations?

Elder David A. Bednar taught: "In some way and at some time, someone in this Church will do or say something that could be considered offensive. Such an event will surely happen to each and every one of us—and it certainly will occur more than once. . . . You and I cannot control the intentions or behavior of other people. However, we do determine how we will act. Please remember that you and I are agents endowed with moral agency, and we can choose not to be offended" ("And Nothing Shall Offend Them," *Ensign* or *Liahona,* Nov. 2006, 91).

See also Proverbs 16:32; Moroni 7:45; David A. Bednar, "Meek and Lowly of Heart," *Ensign* or *Liahona,* May 2018, 30–33.

Ideas for Family Scripture Study and Family Home Evening

As you read the scriptures with your family, the Spirit can help you know what principles to emphasize and discuss in order to meet the needs of your family. Here are some ideas.

Alma 53:10–17. The Anti-Nephi-Lehies covenanted not to shed blood. What covenants have we made with God? What do we read in Alma 53:10–17 that inspires us to be more faithful to our covenants?

Alma 53:20–21. How can we be more like Helaman's young men? It might help to discuss what some of the phrases in these verses mean; for example, what does it mean to be "valiant . . . for strength and activity"? What does it mean to "walk uprightly before [God]"?

Alma 58:9–11, 33, 37. In times of great need, do we turn to Heavenly Father, as the Nephite soldiers did? How did He answer their prayers? How has He answered our prayers?

Alma 61:2, 9, 19. What do we learn from Pahoran about how to respond when we are falsely accused?

Alma 62:39–41. Here's an object lesson that can help your family understand that we can choose to be either "hardened" or "softened" by our trials: Place a raw potato and a raw egg in a pot of boiling water. The potato and the egg represent us, and the water represents the trials we face. As the potato and egg boil, you could talk about some of the trials your family faces. What are some different ways to react to trials like these? According to Alma 62:41, how do our reactions to trials affect us? After the potato and egg are fully cooked, cut open the potato and crack open the egg to show that the same "trial" softened the potato and hardened the egg. What can our family do to be sure that our trials humble us and bring us closer to God?

For more ideas for teaching children, see this week's outline in *Come, Follow Me—For Primary.*

Improving Our Teaching

Let children express their creativity. "When you invite [your] children to create something related to a gospel principle, you help them better understand the principle, and you give them a tangible reminder of what they have learned. . . . Allow them to build, draw, color, write, and create" (*Teaching in the Savior's Way,* 25).

It's True, Sir, All Present and Accounted For, by Clark Kelley Price

Helaman 1–6

"THE ROCK OF OUR REDEEMER"

The principles in this outline can help guide your study of Helaman 1–6, but don't let them limit you. The Holy Ghost will guide you to the truths you need to learn.

RECORD YOUR IMPRESSIONS

The book of Helaman records both triumphs and tragedies among the Nephites and Lamanites. It begins with "a serious difficulty among the people of the Nephites" (Helaman 1:1), and the difficulties keep coming throughout the record. Here we read about political intrigue, bands of robbers, rejection of the prophets, and pride and disbelief throughout the land. But we also find examples like Nephi and Lehi and "the more humble part of the people," who not only survived but thrived spiritually (Helaman 3:34). How did they do it? How did they stay strong while their civilization began to decline and fall apart? The same way any of us stay strong in the "mighty storm" the devil sends to "beat upon [us]"—by building our lives "upon the rock of our Redeemer, who is Christ, the Son of God, . . . a foundation whereon if men build they cannot fall" (Helaman 5:12).

Ideas for Personal Scripture Study

Pride separates me from the Spirit and strength of the Lord.

As you read Helaman 1–6—and throughout the Book of Mormon—you may notice a pattern in the behavior of the Nephites: When the Nephites are righteous, God blesses them and they prosper. After a time, they become prideful and wicked, making choices that lead to destruction and suffering. Then they are humbled and inspired to repent, and God blesses them once again. The pattern repeats itself so often that some people call it the "pride cycle."

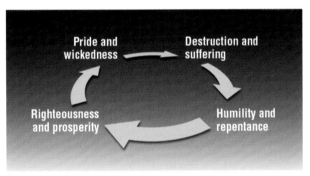

The "pride cycle."

Look for examples of this cycle as you read. You may even want to mark examples when you find them. Here are some questions to help you understand this pattern and see how it might apply to you:

- What evidences of pride do you see among the Nephites? (see, for example, Helaman 3:33–34; 4:11–13). Do you see similar examples of pride in yourself?

- What are the consequences of pride and wickedness? (see Helaman 4:23–26). What are the

consequences of humility and repentance? (see Helaman 3:27–30, 35; 4:14–16).

- What did Helaman want his sons to remember? (see Helaman 5:4–12). How can remembering these truths help you avoid becoming prideful?

See also Dieter F. Uchtdorf, "Pride and the Priesthood," *Ensign* or *Liahona,* Nov. 2010, 55–58.

I can be sanctified as I yield my heart to God.

In Helaman 3, Mormon described a time when the Church was so prosperous and blessed that even the leaders were surprised (see verses 24–32). Eventually some people became prideful, while others grew "stronger and stronger in their humility, . . . even to the purifying and the sanctification of their hearts" (Helaman 3:35). Notice in verses 34–35 what the more humble people did to become sanctified. How do these things help you become more sanctified? It may help to know that the Guide to the Scriptures (scriptures.ChurchofJesusChrist.org) defines *sanctification* as "the process of becoming free from sin, pure, clean, and holy through the Atonement of Jesus Christ." What do you feel inspired to do to follow the example of these disciples? What are you doing to yield your heart to God?

My faith is strengthened by "the greatness of the evidences [I have] received."

Elder Jeffrey R. Holland once said to those who struggle with their faith: "You have more faith than you think you do because of what the Book of Mormon calls 'the greatness of the evidences' [Helaman 5:50]. . . . The fruit of living the gospel is evident in the lives of Latter-day Saints everywhere" ("Lord, I Believe," *Ensign* or *Liahona,* May 2013, 94). As you read these verses, think about evidences that the Lord has given you. For example, maybe you haven't literally heard the Lord's voice, but have you felt "a whisper" from the Holy Ghost that "did pierce even to the very soul"? (Helaman 5:30; see also D&C 88:66). Perhaps you've been in darkness, cried unto God for greater faith, and been "filled with that joy which is unspeakable" (Helaman 5:40–47). What other experiences have strengthened your faith in Christ and His gospel?

Ideas for Family Scripture Study and Family Home Evening

As you read the scriptures with your family, the Spirit can help you know what principles to emphasize and discuss in order to meet the needs of your family. Here are some ideas.

Helaman 3:27–30. As the prophet Mormon abridged the sacred records, he occasionally used the phrase "thus we see" to emphasize important truths. What did he want us to see in Helaman 3:27–30? Throughout your study this week, you might pause occasionally to ask family members how they would complete the phrase "and thus we see" regarding what they have read. What truths do they want to emphasize?

Helaman 5:6–7. President George Albert Smith's deceased grandfather George A. Smith appeared to him in a dream and asked, "I would like to know

what you have done with my name." President Smith responded, "I have never done anything with your name of which you need be ashamed" (in *Teachings of Presidents of the Church: George Albert Smith* [2011], xxvi). After reading Helaman 5:6–7, perhaps you could talk to your family members about remembering and honoring the names we carry, including the name of the Savior.

Helaman 5:12. To help your family visualize what it means to have "a sure foundation," perhaps you could build a small structure together and place it on different kinds of foundations. You could then create a "mighty storm" by spraying water on it and using a fan or hair dryer to create wind. What happened to the structure when it was on the different foundations? How is Jesus Christ like "a sure foundation" in our lives?

Helaman 5:29–33. What experiences have we had with recognizing the voice of God in our lives?

For more ideas for teaching children, see this week's outline in *Come, Follow Me—For Primary.*

Improving Personal Study

Be patient with yourself. A foundation of faith is built one piece at a time. If you find certain doctrines difficult to understand now, be patient. Trust that understanding will come as you build your foundation on Jesus Christ by exercising faith and studying diligently.

© *The Book of Mormon for Young Readers, Nephi and Lehi Encircled by a Pillar of Fire,* by Briana Shawcroft; may not be copied

Illustration of Nephi in a garden tower by Jerry Thompson

AUGUST 24–30

Helaman 7–12

"REMEMBER THE LORD"

Nephi, Lehi, and others had "many revelations daily" (Helaman 11:23). Frequent revelation is not just for prophets—it's available to you, too. Recording your impressions can help you receive revelation more consistently.

RECORD YOUR IMPRESSIONS _____

_____

_____

Nephi's father, Helaman, had urged his sons to "remember, remember": he wanted them to remember their ancestors, remember the words of the prophets, and most of all remember "our Redeemer, who is Christ" (see Helaman 5:5–14). It's clear that Nephi did remember, because this is the same message he declared years later "with unwearyingness" (Helaman 10:4) to the people. "How could you have forgotten your God?" (Helaman 7:20), he asked. All of Nephi's efforts—preaching, praying, performing miracles,

and petitioning God for a famine—were attempts to help the people turn to God and remember Him. In many ways, forgetting God is a bigger problem even than not knowing Him, and it's easy to forget Him when our minds are distracted by "the vain things of this world" and clouded by sin (Helaman 7:21; see also Helaman 12:2). But, as Nephi's ministry shows, it's never too late to remember and "turn . . . unto the Lord your God" (Helaman 7:17).

Ideas for Personal Scripture Study

Prophets reveal the will of God.

There are many prophets described throughout the Book of Mormon, but Helaman 7–11 is a particularly good place to learn what a prophet is, what he does, and how we should receive his words. As you read these chapters, pay attention to Nephi's actions, thoughts, and interactions with the Lord. How does Nephi's ministry help you better understand the role of the prophet in our day? Here are a few examples. What else do you find?

Helaman 7:17–22. Prophets cry repentance and warn of the consequences of sin.

Helaman 7:29; 9:21–36. Prophets know by revelation from God what the people need to hear.

Helaman 10:7. Prophets are given the power to seal on earth and in heaven (see also Matthew 16:19; D&C 132:46).

Helaman 10:4–7, 11–12. _____
_____
_____

How do these verses affect how you feel about our living prophet? What has he taught recently? What are you doing to listen to and follow his direction?

Signs and miracles are helpful but not sufficient to build enduring faith.

If signs or miracles were enough to change a person's heart, then all of the Nephites would have been converted by the remarkable signs Nephi gave in Helaman 9. Instead, "a division among the people" (Helaman 10:1) arose because many of them "did still harden their hearts" (Helaman 10:15). How do the wicked often react to signs and miracles? (see Helaman 10:12–15; see also 3 Nephi 2:1–2). What is the danger of making signs the foundation of a testimony? (see "Signs," Gospel Topics, topics.ChurchofJesusChrist.org).

Pondering invites revelation.

If you have ever felt downtrodden, anxious, or confused, you might learn an important lesson from Nephi's example in Helaman 10:2–4. What did he do when he felt "cast down"? (verse 3).

President Henry B. Eyring taught, "When we ponder, we invite revelation by the Spirit. Pondering, to me, is the thinking and the praying I do after reading and studying in the scriptures carefully" ("Serve with the Spirit," *Ensign* or *Liahona,* Nov. 2010, 60). How might you create a habit of pondering? To read about one way to regularly ponder the word of God, see Brother Devin G. Durrant's message "My Heart Pondereth Them Continually" (*Ensign* or *Liahona,* Nov. 2015, 112–15).

See also Proverbs 4:26; Luke 2:19; 1 Nephi 11:1; 2 Nephi 4:15–16; 3 Nephi 17:3; Moroni 10:3; D&C 88:62.

The Lord wants me to remember Him.

In Helaman 12, Mormon, who was abridging the record, summarizes some of the lessons we can learn from the account of Nephi in the previous chapters. Consider using his summary as an opportunity to examine your own heart. You might even make a list of the things Mormon says cause people to forget the Lord. What helps you remember Him? What changes are you inspired to make based on what you learned?

Ideas for Family Scripture Study and Family Home Evening

As you read the scriptures with your family, the Spirit can help you know what principles to emphasize and discuss in order to meet the needs of your family. Here are some ideas.

Helaman 7–9. What similarities do we see between things that Nephi did and what prophets do today? What is our prophet teaching today? Perhaps you could choose some recent counsel the prophet has given and discuss as a family ways you can better follow it.

Helaman 10:4–5, 11–12. How did Nephi demonstrate that he sought the Lord's will rather than his own? How can we follow his example? What are some ways our family can better seek the Lord's will?

Helaman 11:1–16. What did Nephi desire and what did he do about it? What do we learn about prayer from Nephi's example?

Helaman 11:17–23. What do we learn about Nephi's brother, Lehi, in Helaman 11:17–23? Whom do we know who lives a righteous life without receiving a lot of recognition?

Helaman 12:1–6. Can you think of an object lesson you can use to help your family understand what "unsteadiness" means? For instance, you might invite a family member to try balancing something on his or her head. You could then invite family members to look in Helaman 12:1–6 for reasons people can be unsteady in following the Lord. How can we remain spiritually steady?

For more ideas for teaching children, see this week's outline in *Come, Follow Me—For Primary*.

Improving Our Teaching

Review. Here's an idea to help family members remember the scriptures they are learning: Select a verse you find meaningful, and display it in your home where family members will see it often. Invite other family members to take turns selecting a scripture to display, and discuss it when the family gathers, such as at meals or family prayer.

© *The Book of Mormon for Young Readers, Seantum—The Murderer Is Discovered,* by Briana Shawcroft; may not be copied

Samuel the Lamanite on the Wall, by Arnold Friberg

AUGUST 31–SEPTEMBER 6

Helaman 13–16

"GLAD TIDINGS OF GREAT JOY"

As you record your impressions this week, think about how the principles in Helaman 13–16 build on and reinforce other things you have been learning in the scriptures.

RECORD YOUR IMPRESSIONS_____

_____

_____

The first time Samuel the Lamanite tried to share "glad tidings" in Zarahemla (Helaman 13:7), he was rejected and cast out by the hard-hearted Nephites. You might say it was as if they had built an impenetrable wall around their hearts that prevented them from receiving Samuel's message. Samuel understood the importance of the message he bore and demonstrated faith by following God's commandment "that he should return again, and prophesy" (Helaman 13:3). Just as Samuel did, we all encounter walls as we "prepare the way of the Lord" (Helaman 14:9) and strive to follow His prophets. And like Samuel, we too bear witness of Jesus Christ, "who surely shall come," and invite all to "believe on his name" (Helaman 13:6; 14:13). Not everyone will listen, and some may actively oppose us. But those who believe in this message with faith in Christ find that it truly is "glad tidings of great joy" (Helaman 16:14).

Ideas for Personal Scripture Study

HELAMAN 13

The Lord gives warnings through His prophets.

In the scriptures, prophets are sometimes compared to watchmen on a wall or tower who warn of dangers (see Isaiah 62:6; Ezekiel 33:1–7).

President M. Russell Ballard taught: "Through the centuries, prophets have fulfilled their duty when they have warned people of the dangers before them. The Lord's Apostles are duty bound to watch, warn, and reach out to help those seeking answers to life's questions" ("God Is at the Helm," *Ensign* or *Liahona,* Nov. 2015, 25).

As you study and ponder Helaman 13, you could mark the many warnings that Samuel gave. For example, what did he teach about repentance? about humility and wealth? How might these warnings apply to you? What warnings have modern prophets given recently, and what do you feel you should do about those warnings?

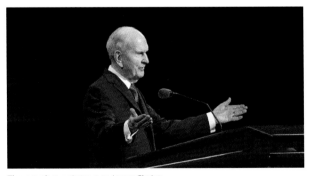

The prophet points us to Jesus Christ.

HELAMAN 13–15

The Lord is merciful to those who repent.

Originally, Samuel was sent to the Nephites to share the joyful news of the Savior's coming (see Helaman 13:7). Because they rejected him, he returned with stern warnings of the judgments of God. But those warnings consistently included a merciful invitation to repent; look for these invitations throughout Helaman 13–15 (see especially Helaman 13:6, 11; 14:15–19; 15:7–8). How do these invitations apply to you? What do you learn from these verses about repentance? When have you experienced the mercy of God that comes from repentance?

HELAMAN 14; 16:13–23

Signs and wonders can strengthen the faith of those who do not harden their hearts.

In Helaman 14, Samuel explained the reason the Lord provided signs of the Savior's birth and death: "To the intent that ye might believe on his name" (Helaman 14:12). As you study Helaman 14, note the signs of the Savior's birth in verses 1–8 and the signs of His death in verses 20–28. Why do you think these signs would be effective ways to signify the birth and death of Jesus Christ?

Can you think of any signs the Lord has given to help you believe in Him? For instance, prophets have predicted signs that will appear before the Savior's Second Coming (see "Signs of the Times," Guide to the Scriptures, scriptures.ChurchofJesusChrist.org). Have any of these signs been fulfilled in our day? Other signs that lead to faith in Jesus Christ may be more personal and less dramatic. Take a moment to ponder ways you have witnessed His hand in your life.

What caution is given about signs in Helaman 16:13–23? How can you avoid the attitude of the people described in these verses?

See also Alma 30:43–52; Ronald A. Rasband, "By Divine Design," *Ensign* or *Liahona,* Nov. 2017, 55–57.

HELAMAN 16

Following the prophet's counsel brings me closer to the Lord.

Elder Neil L. Andersen taught: "I have found that as I prayerfully study the words of the prophet of God and carefully, with patience, spiritually align my will with his inspired teachings, my faith in the Lord Jesus Christ always increases. If we choose to set his counsel aside and determine that we know better, our faith suffers and our eternal perspective is clouded" ("The Prophet of God," *Ensign* or *Liahona,* May 2018, 26–27). How do the words and actions of the Nephites in Helaman 16 confirm what Elder Andersen taught? What personal commitments do you feel you should make regarding the Lord's prophets and their messages?

Ideas for Family Scripture Study and Family Home Evening

As you read the scriptures with your family, the Spirit can help you know what principles to emphasize and discuss in order to meet the needs of your family. Here are some ideas.

Helaman 13:3–4. What inspires your family about Samuel's response to the Lord's command in

Helaman 13:3–4? During your family study this week, perhaps you could encourage family members to share impressions that "come into [their] heart."

Helaman 13:38. The idea that happiness can be found "in doing iniquity" is common in our day. In what ways has living the gospel brought us true happiness?

Helaman 15:3. How does God's correction show His love for us? Invite family members to humbly ask the Lord what they can do to improve.

Helaman 15:5–8. What do we learn about conversion from the Lamanites described in these verses? How can we follow their example?

Helaman 16:1–3. Would your family enjoy acting out the story of Samuel the Lamanite? After reading the account, maybe family members could take turns standing on a chair and reading some of Samuel's prophecies while other family members pretend to shoot arrows or throw stones. This could help your family understand how Samuel and the Nephites may have felt. Young children might also enjoy drawing pictures of the story. How can we be like Samuel and share the gospel with others despite our fears?

For more ideas for teaching children, see this week's outline in *Come, Follow Me—For Primary.*

Improving Personal Study

Look for patterns. A pattern is a plan or model that can be used as a guide for accomplishing a task. In the scriptures, we find patterns that show how the Lord accomplishes His work, such as sending His servants to warn the people.

© *The Book of Mormon for Young Readers, Samuel the Lamanite,* by Briana Shawcroft; may not be copied

One Day, One Night, and One Day, by Jorge Cocco

3 Nephi 1–7

"LIFT UP YOUR HEAD AND BE OF GOOD CHEER"

The Nephites witnessed miraculous signs, but over time they forgot what they had experienced (see 3 Nephi 2:1). Recording your impressions will help you remember your spiritual experiences while studying 3 Nephi 1–7.

RECORD YOUR IMPRESSIONS

In some ways, it was an exciting time to be a believer in Jesus Christ. Prophecies were being fulfilled—great signs and miracles among the people indicated that the Savior would soon be born. On the other hand, it was also an anxious time for believers because, in spite of all the miracles, unbelievers insisted that "the time was past" for the Savior to be born (3 Nephi 1:5). These people caused "a great uproar throughout the land" (3 Nephi 1:7) and even set a date to kill all the believers if the sign prophesied by Samuel the Lamanite—a night without darkness—did not appear.

In these trying circumstances, the prophet Nephi "cried mightily to his God in behalf of his people" (3 Nephi 1:11). The Lord's response is inspiring to anyone who faces persecution or doubt and needs to know that light will overcome darkness: "Lift up your head and be of good cheer; . . . I will fulfil all that which I have caused to be spoken by the mouth of my holy prophets" (3 Nephi 1:13).

Ideas for Personal Scripture Study

3 NEPHI 1:4–21; 5:1–3

The Lord will fulfill all His words.

How do you imagine you would have felt if you had been one of the believers during the time described in 3 Nephi 1–7? How might it have felt, for example, to wait for the night with no darkness that would announce the Savior's birth, knowing you would be killed if it didn't happen? As you read 3 Nephi 1:4–21 and 5:1–3, look for what Nephi and the other believers did to keep their faith during these difficult times. How did the Lord bless them? What do you learn that can help when you find yourself waiting for blessings promised by the Lord?

3 NEPHI 1:22; 2:1–3

Forgetting spiritual experiences makes me vulnerable to Satan's temptations.

You might think that witnessing something so miraculous as a night without darkness would stay with you for a long time and be an anchor to your testimony. But the memories of the signs and wonders the Nephites witnessed seemed to fade over time. What caused them to forget, and what were the results of forgetting? (see 3 Nephi 1:22; 2:1–3).

What are you doing to remember and renew your witness of spiritual truths? For example, consider how recording your spiritual experiences can help you. How will you share your witness with those closest to you to help them believe?

See also Alma 5:6; Henry B. Eyring, "O Remember, Remember," *Ensign* or *Liahona,* Nov. 2007, 66–69;

Neil L. Andersen, "Faith Is Not by Chance, but by Choice," *Ensign* or *Liahona,* Nov. 2015, 65–68.

3 NEPHI 2:11–12; 3:1–26; 5:24–26

The Lord strengthens His Saints against spiritual danger.

In our day, we usually don't face bands of robbers that force us to leave our homes and gather in one place. But we do face spiritual dangers, and the Nephites' experience may contain lessons that can help us. Look for these lessons as you read 3 Nephi 2:11–12 and 3:1–26.

In 3 Nephi 5:24–26 we read of the gathering of the Lord's people in the latter days. What do these verses teach about how the Lord is gathering His people today?

See also "Worldwide Devotional for Youth: Messages from President Russell M. Nelson and Sister Wendy W. Nelson," June 3, 2018, ChurchofJesusChrist.org; "Israel—The gathering of Israel," Guide to the Scriptures, scriptures.ChurchofJesusChrist.org.

3 NEPHI 5:12–26; 7:15–26

I am a disciple of Jesus Christ.

What do you think it means to be a disciple of Jesus Christ? (see D&C 41:5). In 3 Nephi 5:12–26, Mormon interrupted his abridgment of the Nephite records and declared that he was a disciple of Jesus Christ. Then, in 3 Nephi 7:15–26, he described the ministry of another disciple—the prophet Nephi. What do you find in these two passages that helps you understand what it means to be a disciple of Christ?

Ideas for Family Scripture Study and Family Home Evening

As you read the scriptures with your family, the Spirit can help you know what principles to emphasize and discuss in order to meet the needs of your family. Here are some ideas.

3 Nephi 3:13–14, 25–26. What did the Nephites do to protect themselves from the enemy they faced? What are we doing to make our home a place of safety and protection from the evil in the world?

3 Nephi 2:1–3; 6:15–17. To help your family learn how Satan can deceive us, draw a body, and as your family reads 3 Nephi 2:1–3 and 6:15–17, mark the different parts of the body mentioned. According to these verses, what are some of the ways Satan tempts us to forget God and turn to sin?

3 Nephi 4:7–12, 30–33. What did the Nephites do when they saw the Gadianton robbers coming? What can our family learn from the Nephites when we face difficult situations? What can we learn from the Nephites' words after the Lord helped them in their time of difficulty?

3 Nephi 5:13; Doctrine and Covenants 41:5. Read 3 Nephi 5:13 and Doctrine and Covenants 41:5, and discuss what it means to be a disciple of Christ. Maybe family members could talk about times when they noticed each other being disciples. If you have small children, you might make a badge that says, "I am a disciple of Jesus Christ," and let them wear the badge whenever you notice them following the Savior.

For more ideas for teaching children, see this week's outline in *Come, Follow Me—For Primary*.

Improving Our Teaching

Help your family liken the scriptures to themselves. Nephi said, "I did liken all scriptures unto us, that it might be for our profit and learning" (1 Nephi 19:23). To help your family liken the scriptures to themselves, you could invite them to ponder what they would have done if they had been among the believers described in 3 Nephi 1:4–9. (See *Teaching in the Savior's Way*, 21.)

A Day, a Night, and a Day, by Walter Rane

I Am the Light of the World, by James Fullmer

3 Nephi 8–11

"ARISE AND COME FORTH UNTO ME"

In 3 Nephi 8–11, the people heard the voice of God speaking to them. As you read these chapters, pay attention to what His voice says to you.

RECORD YOUR IMPRESSIONS

"Behold, I am Jesus Christ, whom the prophets testified shall come into the world" (3 Nephi 11:10). With these words, the resurrected Savior introduced Himself, fulfilling over 600 years of Book of Mormon prophecies. "That appearance and that declaration," Elder Jeffrey R. Holland wrote, "constituted the focal point, the supreme moment, in the entire history of the Book of Mormon. It was the manifestation and the decree that had informed and inspired every Nephite prophet. . . . Everyone had talked of him, sung of him, dreamed of him, and prayed for his appearance—but here he actually was. The day of days! The God who turns every dark night into morning light had arrived" (*Christ and the New Covenant* [1997], 250–51).

Ideas for Personal Scripture Study

3 NEPHI 8–11

Jesus Christ is the Light of the World.

You might notice that themes related to darkness and light—both physical and spiritual—are repeated throughout 3 Nephi 8–11. What do you learn from these chapters about spiritual darkness and light? What brings darkness into your life? What brings light? Why do you think the Savior chose to introduce Himself as "the light and the life of the world"?

(3 Nephi 9:18; 11:11). How has Jesus Christ been a light in your life?

If I repent, the Savior will gather, protect, and heal me.

How do you imagine the people felt after experiencing the destruction and darkness described in 3 Nephi 8? How do you think they may have felt when they heard the Savior's voice speaking about light, mercy, and redemption in chapters 9 and 10?

Even though the Savior proclaimed that the terrible destruction was a result of the people's sins, He promised that he would heal those who would return to Him and repent (see 3 Nephi 9:2, 13). Elder Neil L. Andersen remarked: "I am amazed at the Savior's encircling arms of mercy and love for the repentant, no matter how selfish the forsaken sin. I testify that the Savior is able and eager to forgive our sins" ("Repent . . . That I May Heal You," *Ensign* or *Liahona,* Nov. 2009, 40).

Search 3 Nephi 9–10 for evidence of Christ's mercy and His eagerness to forgive. For example, what do you find in 3 Nephi 9:13–22 and 10:1–6 that helps you feel the Savior's love and mercy? Ponder experiences when you have felt Him "gather" and "nourish" you (see 3 Nephi 10:4). Consider recording these experiences in a journal or sharing them with your loved ones.

I can learn to hear and understand God's voice.

Have you ever felt that you were struggling to understand a message that God was communicating to you? Perhaps the experience of the people in 3 Nephi 11:1–8 can help you understand some principles of hearing and understanding God's voice. You might note the characteristics of God's voice that the people heard and what they did to better understand it. How might this account apply to your efforts to hear and recognize the voice of God in your life through personal revelation?

Jesus Christ invites me to gain a personal testimony of Him.

There were about 2,500 people gathered in Bountiful when Jesus Christ appeared (see 3 Nephi 17:25). Despite this large number, the Savior invited them each "one by one" to feel the nail prints in His hands and feet (3 Nephi 11:14–15). What does this suggest to you about the importance of having personal experiences that build faith in Jesus Christ? In what ways does the Savior invite you to "arise and come forth unto" Him? (3 Nephi 11:14). What experiences have helped you gain a witness that He is your Savior? You might also consider how the Savior's example in these verses could inspire your efforts to minister to others.

One by One, by Walter Rane

Ideas for Family Scripture Study and Family Home Evening

As you read the scriptures with your family, the Spirit can help you know what principles to emphasize and discuss in order to meet the needs of your family. Here are some ideas.

3 Nephi 8–9. To help your family relate to the experiences described in 3 Nephi 8–9, you could retell or listen to a recording of portions of these chapters in a darkened room. Discuss what it might have been like to be in darkness for three days. Then you could talk about how Jesus Christ is "the light . . . of the world" (3 Nephi 9:18).

3 Nephi 10:1–6. The imagery of a hen gathering her chicks can be a powerful teaching tool to help children understand the Savior's character and mission. You could read these verses while your family looks at a picture of a hen and chicks. Why would a hen need to gather her chicks? Why does the Savior want to gather us close to Him? What might happen if a chick chose not to gather when called?

3 Nephi 11:1–7. Perhaps you could read some of these verses in a soft, "small voice" (3 Nephi 11:3). What did the people have to do to understand the voice from heaven? What do we learn from their experience?

3 Nephi 11:21–38. Is someone in your family preparing to be baptized? Reading 3 Nephi 11:21–38 could help them prepare. How can pondering the Savior's teachings in these verses help family members who have already been baptized?

3 Nephi 11:29–30. What do these verses teach us about contention? How can we "[do] away" with contention in our home? (3 Nephi 11:30).

For more ideas for teaching children, see this week's outline in *Come, Follow Me—For Primary.*

Improving Personal Study

Record impressions. Elder Richard G. Scott said, "Knowledge carefully recorded is knowledge available in time of need. . . . [Recording spiritual impressions] enhances the likelihood of your receiving further light" ("Acquiring Spiritual Knowledge," *Ensign,* Nov. 1993, 88).

One Shepherd, by Howard Lyon

Third Nephi: These Twelve Whom I Have Chosen, by Gary L. Kapp

3 Nephi 12–16

"I AM THE LAW, AND THE LIGHT"

There are many principles to find in 3 Nephi 12–16. Some are highlighted in this outline, but you may find others. Let Heavenly Father, through His Spirit, teach you what you need right now.

RECORD YOUR IMPRESSIONS

Like Jesus's disciples who gathered at the mount in Galilee, the people who gathered at the temple at Bountiful had lived under the law of Moses. They had followed it because it pointed their souls to Christ (see Jacob 4:5), and now Christ stood before them, declaring a higher law. But even those of us who have never lived the law of Moses can recognize that the standard Jesus set for His disciples is a much higher law. "I would that ye should be perfect," He declared (3 Nephi 12:48). If this makes you feel inadequate, remember that Jesus also said, "Blessed are the poor in spirit who come unto me, for theirs is the kingdom of heaven" (3 Nephi 12:3). This higher law is an invitation—another way of saying "Come unto me and be ye saved" (3 Nephi 12:20). Like the law of Moses, this law points us to Christ—the only One who can save and perfect us. "Behold," He said, "I am the law, and the light. Look unto me, and endure to the end, and ye shall live" (3 Nephi 15:9).

Ideas for Personal Scripture Study

3 NEPHI 12–14

The Savior's teachings show me how to be a true disciple.

There are many truths, words of counsel, and warnings in 3 Nephi 12–14. Here's one way to study and apply what the Savior taught in these chapters: Pick a group of verses, and see if you can summarize what the verses teach in one sentence that begins with "True disciples of Jesus Christ . . ." For example, a summary of 3 Nephi 14:1–5 might be "True disciples of Jesus Christ are not judgmental." You might want to choose a verse from these chapters that is especially meaningful to you and memorize it or copy it and place it where you will see it often. Ponder how you can apply what you learn to your personal efforts to be a better disciple of Jesus Christ.

See also Matthew 5–7; Luke 6:20–49.

3 NEPHI 12:1–2; 15:23–24; 16:1–6

Blessed are those who believe without seeing.

Compared to the total number of God's children, very few have seen the Savior and heard His voice, as the people at Bountiful did. Most of us are more like the people described in 3 Nephi 12:2; 15:23; and 16:4–6. What promises are made to such people in these verses? How have these promises been fulfilled in your life?

See also John 20:26–29; 2 Nephi 26:12–13; Alma 32:16–18.

3 NEPHI 12:21–30; 13:1–8, 16–18; 14:21–23

Righteous acts are not enough; my heart must also be pure.

One theme you might notice in these chapters is the Savior's invitation to live a higher law—to be righteous not only in our outward actions but also in our hearts. Look for this theme when the Savior speaks of contention (3 Nephi 12:21–26), immorality (3 Nephi 12:27–30), prayer (3 Nephi 13:5–8), and fasting (3 Nephi 13:16–18). What other examples can you find? What can you do to purify the desires of your heart rather than focus on outward actions only?

3 NEPHI 14:7–11

If I seek "good things" from Heavenly Father, I will receive.

President Russell M. Nelson said: "Does God really *want* to speak to you? Yes! . . . Oh, there is so much more that your Father in Heaven wants you to know" ("Revelation for the Church, Revelation for Our Lives," *Ensign* or *Liahona,* May 2018, 95). As you read the Lord's invitation in 3 Nephi 14:7–11 to ask, seek, and knock, ponder what "good things" He might want you to ask for. The following additional scriptures may help you understand how to ask, seek, and knock. They may also help explain why some prayers are not answered the way you expect: Isaiah 55:8–9; Helaman 10:5; Moroni 7:26–27, 33, 37; and Doctrine and Covenants 9:7–9.

Ideas for Family Scripture Study and Family Home Evening

As you read the scriptures with your family, the Spirit can help you know what principles to emphasize and discuss in order to meet the needs of your family. Here are some ideas.

3 Nephi 12:48. How does Elder Jeffrey R. Holland's message "Be Ye Therefore Perfect—Eventually" (*Ensign* or *Liahona*, Nov. 2017, 40–42) help us understand the Savior's words in this verse? You could also find help in Moroni 10:32–33.

3 Nephi 12:9, 38–42; 14:3–5, 12. How do these verses apply to interactions among family members? Perhaps your family could set some goals together to live by these principles more faithfully.

3 Nephi 13:19–21. These verses could prompt a discussion about what your family treasures. Are there some treasures on earth that are keeping you from laying up treasures in heaven? You could reinforce this point by leading the family on a treasure hunt to find things in your home that remind your family members of treasures with eternal value.

3 Nephi 14:7–11. Younger children might enjoy a game, inspired by 3 Nephi 14:8–9, in which they ask for something and receive something entirely different. What did the Savior want us to know about our Father in Heaven when He shared this example?

3 Nephi 14:15–20. What "good fruit" helps us know that Joseph Smith, or the current President of the Church, is a true prophet?

3 Nephi 14:24–27. Think of ways you could help your family visualize the parable in these verses. Perhaps family members could draw pictures, do actions, or build things on solid and sandy foundations.

For more ideas for teaching children, see this week's outline in *Come, Follow Me—For Primary.*

Improving Our Teaching

Use object lessons. The Savior taught profound truths by referring to familiar objects. You could do something similar as your family reads 3 Nephi 12–16. For example, when you read chapter 12, you could show some salt, a candle, and a coat. This could also lead to a good review activity. After you've read these chapters, display the objects again, and ask family members what the Savior taught about each.

The Savior's Visit to the People in America, by Glen S. Hopkinson

The Light of His Countenance Did Shine upon Them, by Gary L. Kapp

SEPTEMBER 28–OCTOBER 11

3 Nephi 17–19

"BEHOLD, MY JOY IS FULL"

While previous chapters in 3 Nephi focused mainly on the Savior's words, chapters 17–19 describe His ministry and teachings among the people. As you read these chapters, what does the Spirit teach you about the Savior?

RECORD YOUR IMPRESSIONS _____

_____

_____

Jesus Christ had just spent the day ministering in the land of Bountiful, teaching His gospel, giving the people a chance to see and feel the marks in His resurrected body, and testifying that He was the promised Savior. And now it was time for Him to leave. He needed to return to His Father, and He knew that the people needed time to ponder what He had taught. So promising to return the next day, He dismissed the multitude to their homes. But no one left. They didn't say what they were feeling, but Jesus could sense it: they hoped He would "tarry a little longer with them" (3 Nephi 17:5). He had other important things to do, but the opportunity to show compassion does not always come at a convenient time, so Jesus stayed with the people a little longer. What followed was perhaps the most tender example of ministering recorded in scripture. Those who were present could only say it was indescribable (see 3 Nephi 17:16–17). Jesus Himself summed up the impromptu spiritual outpouring with these simple words: "Now behold, my joy is full" (3 Nephi 17:20).

Ideas for Personal Scripture Study

The Savior is my perfect example of ministering.

We know that there were about 2,500 people (see 3 Nephi 17:25) who experienced Christ's first visit, as recorded in 3 Nephi 11–18. Yet the Savior found a way to minister to them one by one. What do you learn about ministering from the Savior's example in this chapter? What needs did He minister to? Ponder how His example can help you minister to others.

Behold Your Little Ones, by Gary L. Kapp

The Savior taught us how to pray.

Imagine what it would be like to hear the Savior pray for you. What might He say in your behalf? His teachings and prayers in these chapters might give you an idea. As you study, what do you learn from Christ's example that can make your own prayers more meaningful? What blessings from prayer have you seen in your life?

I can be spiritually filled as I partake of the sacrament.

As you read 3 Nephi 18:1–12, ponder how taking the sacrament can help you be spiritually "filled" (3 Nephi 18:3–5, 9; see also 3 Nephi 20:1–9). For example, you could make a list of questions to prompt personal reflection when you take the sacrament, such as "How do I feel about the Savior and His sacrifice for me?" "How is His sacrifice influencing my daily life?" or "What am I doing well as a disciple, and what can I improve?"

These words from President Henry B. Eyring may help you ponder one way the sacrament can help you be spiritually filled: "As you examine your life during the ordinance of the sacrament, I hope your thoughts center not only on things you have done wrong but also on things you have done right—moments when you have felt that Heavenly Father and the Savior were pleased with you. You may even take a moment during the sacrament to ask God to help you see these things. . . . When I have done this, the Spirit has reassured me that while I'm still far from perfect, I'm better today than I was yesterday. And this gives me confidence that, because of the Savior, I can be even better tomorrow" ("Always Remember Him," *Ensign,* Feb. 2018, 5).

Disciples of Jesus Christ seek the gift of the Holy Ghost.

Think about a prayer you said recently. What do your prayers teach you about your deepest desires? After spending a day in the presence of the Savior, the multitude "did pray for that which they most desired"—the gift of the Holy Ghost (3 Nephi 19:9). As you read these passages, ponder your own desire for the companionship of the Holy Ghost. What do you learn about seeking the companionship of the Holy Ghost?

Ideas for Family Scripture Study and Family Home Evening

As you read the scriptures with your family, the Spirit can help you know what principles to emphasize and discuss in order to meet the needs of your family. Here are some ideas.

3 Nephi 17. As you read this chapter as a family, consider pausing from time to time to invite your family to imagine experiencing these events first-hand. For example, you might ask questions like "What afflictions would you bring to the Savior to be healed?" "What would you want Him to pray for in your behalf?" or "What loved ones would you want Him to bless?" Reading this chapter may also inspire you to pray for your family members, one by one, as Jesus did.

3 Nephi 18:1–12. What does it mean to be "filled" by partaking of the sacrament, and how do we experience it? What do we learn from verses 5–7 about why Jesus gave us the ordinance of the sacrament?

3 Nephi 18:17–21. What do we learn from these verses about the purposes of prayer? How can we improve the spiritual power of our prayers, both as individuals and as a family?

3 Nephi 18:25; 19:1–3. What has our family experienced through the gospel that we wish everyone around us could also experience? How can we follow the example of the people in these verses and "labor exceedingly" (3 Nephi 19:3) to bring others to Christ, that they too might "feel and see" (3 Nephi 18:25) what we have found in the gospel?

For more ideas for teaching children, see this week's outline in *Come, Follow Me—For Primary*.

Improving Personal Study

Let the Spirit guide your study. The Holy Ghost can guide you toward the things you need to learn each day. Be sensitive to His promptings, even if they seem to suggest that you read a different topic or study in a different way than you usually would. For example, as you read about the sacrament in 3 Nephi 18, the Spirit might prompt you to spend more time on that topic than you planned.

They Saw the Heavens Open, by Walter Rane

Illustration of Christ appearing to the Nephites by Andrew Bosley

3 Nephi 20–26

"YE ARE THE CHILDREN OF THE COVENANT"

When speaking of the scriptures, Jesus often used the word *search* (see 3 Nephi 20:11; 23:1, 5). When you read 3 Nephi 20–26, what will you search for?

RECORD YOUR IMPRESSIONS

When you hear people use terms like *house of Israel,* do you feel like they're talking about you? The Nephites and Lamanites were literal descendants of Israel—their story even begins in Jerusalem—but to some of them, Jerusalem must have seemed like "a land which is far distant, a land which we know not" (Helaman 16:20). Yes, they were "a branch of the tree of Israel," but they were also "lost from its body" (Alma 26:36; see also 1 Nephi 15:12). But when the Savior appeared to them, He wanted them to know that they were not lost to Him. "Ye are of the house of Israel," He said, "and ye are of the covenant" (3 Nephi 20:25). He might say something similar to you today, for anyone who is baptized and makes covenants with Him is also of the house of Israel, "of the covenant," no matter who you descend from or where you live. In other words, when Jesus speaks of the house of Israel, He is talking about you. The instruction to bless "all the kindreds of the earth" is for you (3 Nephi 20:27). The invitation to "awake again, and put on thy strength" is for you (3 Nephi 20:36). And His precious promise, "My kindness shall not depart from thee, neither shall the covenant of my peace be removed," is for you (3 Nephi 22:10).

Ideas for Personal Scripture Study

In the latter days, God will perform a great and marvelous work.

The Savior gave the multitude some remarkable promises and prophesied about the future of His covenant people—and that includes you. As President Russell M. Nelson said: "We are among the covenant people of the Lord. Ours is the privilege to participate personally in the fulfillment of these promises. What an exciting time to live!" ("The Gathering of Scattered Israel," *Ensign* or *Liahona,* Nov. 2006, 79).

Look for prophecies about the last days in the Savior's words in 3 Nephi 20–22. Which of these prophecies are especially exciting to you? What can you do to help fulfill the prophecies in these chapters?

Note that 3 Nephi 21:1–7 indicates that the coming forth of the Book of Mormon ("these things" in verses 2 and 3) is a sign that God's promises have already begun to be fulfilled. What are those promises, and how does the Book of Mormon help fulfill them?

See also Russell M. Nelson, "Hope of Israel" (worldwide devotional for youth, June 3, 2018), broadcasts.ChurchofJesusChrist.org.

The Savior wants me to search the words of the prophets.

Jesus's words and actions throughout these chapters reveal how He feels about the scriptures. What do you learn about the scriptures in 3 Nephi 20:10–12; 23; and 26:1–12? What do you find in these verses that inspires you to "search these things diligently"? (3 Nephi 23:1).

God is merciful to those who return to Him.

In 3 Nephi 22 and 24, the Savior quotes words from Isaiah and Malachi that are full of vivid images and comparisons—colorful foundation stones, coals in the fire, purified silver, the windows of heaven. It might be interesting to make a list of them. What does each one teach you about God's relationship with His people? For example, 3 Nephi 22:4–8 compares God to a husband and His people to a wife. Reading about these images might prompt you to think about your own relationship with the Lord. How have the promises in these chapters been fulfilled in your life? (see especially 3 Nephi 22:7–8, 10–17; 24:10–12, 17–18).

My heart should turn to my ancestors.

The promised return of Elijah has been eagerly anticipated by Jews around the world for centuries. Latter-day Saints know that Elijah has returned, appearing to Joseph Smith in the Kirtland Temple in 1836 (see D&C 110:13–16). The work of turning hearts to the fathers—temple and family history work—is well underway. What experiences have you had that helped turn your heart to your ancestors?

Ideas for Family Scripture Study and Family Home Evening

As you read the scriptures with your family, the Spirit can help you know what principles to emphasize and discuss in order to meet the needs of your family. Here are some ideas.

3 Nephi 22:2. After reading this verse, maybe you could make a homemade tent and talk about how the Church is like a tent in a wilderness. What might it mean to "lengthen [its] cords" and "strengthen

[its] stakes"? How do we invite others to find "shelter" in the Church? (see the video "Welcome" on ComeuntoChrist.org).

3 Nephi 23:6–13. If the Savior were to examine the records our family has kept, what questions might He ask us? Are there any important events or spiritual experiences that we should record? Now might be a good time to create or add to a family record and counsel together about what to include. Younger family members might enjoy decorating your record with photographs or drawings. Why is it important to record our family's spiritual experiences?

3 Nephi 24:7–18. How have we experienced the blessings of paying tithing promised in these verses? Elder David A. Bednar's message "The Windows of Heaven" (*Ensign* or *Liahona*, Nov. 2013, 17–20) could help family members recognize these blessings.

3 Nephi 25:5–6. How will you help your family members turn their hearts to their fathers? Maybe you could assign family members to learn about one of your ancestors and share with the rest of the family what they learn (see FamilySearch.org). Or you could work together to find an ancestor who needs temple ordinances and plan a temple trip to perform those ordinances.

For more ideas for teaching children, see this week's outline in *Come, Follow Me—For Primary.*

Improving Our Teaching

Live your testimony. "You teach what you are," Elder Neal A. Maxwell taught. "Your traits will be more remembered . . . than a particular truth in a particular lesson" ("But a Few Days" [address to Church Educational System religious educators, Sept. 10, 1982], 2). If you want to teach a gospel principle, do your best to live that principle.

Bring Forth the Record, by Gary L. Kapp

Christ's Prayer, by Derek Hegsted

3 Nephi 27–4 Nephi

"THERE COULD NOT BE A HAPPIER PEOPLE"

The Lord commanded His disciples to write the things they experienced (see 3 Nephi 27:23–24). As you study, write down the spiritual experiences you have.

RECORD YOUR IMPRESSIONS

The teachings of Jesus Christ are not just a beautiful philosophy to ponder. They are much more than that—they are meant to change our lives. The book of 4 Nephi provides a stunning example of this, illustrating just how thoroughly the Savior's gospel can transform a people. Following Jesus's brief ministry, centuries of contention between the Nephites and Lamanites came to an end. Two nations known for dissension and pride became "one, the children of Christ" (4 Nephi 1:17), and they began to have "all things common among them" (4 Nephi 1:3). The "love of God . . . did dwell in the hearts of the people," and "there could not be a happier people among all the people who had been created by the hand of God" (4 Nephi 1:15–16). This is how the Savior's teachings changed the Nephites and the Lamanites. How are they changing you?

Ideas for Personal Scripture Study

3 NEPHI 27:1–12

The Church of Jesus Christ is called in His name.

As the Savior's disciples began establishing His Church throughout the land, a question arose that, to some, might seem like a minor point—what should be the name of the Church? (see 3 Nephi 27:1–3). What do you learn about the importance of this name from the Savior's answer in 3 Nephi 27:4–12? In 1838 the Lord revealed the name of His Church today (see D&C 115:4). Ponder each word in that name. How do these words help us know who we are, what we believe, and how we should act?

See also Russell M. Nelson, "The Correct Name of the Church," *Ensign* or *Liahona,* Nov. 2018, 87–80; M. Russell Ballard, "The Importance of a Name," *Ensign* or *Liahona,* Nov. 2011, 79–82.

3 NEPHI 28:1–11

As I purify my desires, I become a more faithful disciple.

What would you say if the Savior asked you, as He asked His disciples, "What is it that ye desire of me?" (3 Nephi 28:1). Think about this as you read about the experience of the Savior's disciples in 3 Nephi 28:1–11. What do you learn about the desires of the disciples' hearts from their answers to His question? President Dallin H. Oaks taught: "To achieve our eternal destiny, we will desire and work for the qualities required to become an eternal being. . . . We will desire to become like [Jesus Christ]" ("Desire," *Ensign* or *Liahona,* May 2011, 44–45). What can you do to make the desires of your heart more righteous? (For more information about the "change wrought upon [the] bodies" of the three disciples, see

3 Nephi 28:37 and "Translated Beings," Guide to the Scriptures, scriptures.ChurchofJesusChrist.org.)

4 NEPHI 1:1–18

Conversion to Jesus Christ and His gospel leads to unity and happiness.

Can you imagine what it would have been like to live in the years following the Savior's visit? How did the people maintain this divine peace for so long—nearly 200 years? As you study 4 Nephi 1:1–18, consider marking or noting the choices that people made in order to experience this blessed life.

Ponder what you can do to help your family, ward, or community live in greater unity and happiness, as the people in 4 Nephi did. What teachings of Jesus Christ can you live more fully in order to accomplish this goal? What can you do to help others understand and live these teachings?

4 NEPHI 1:19–49

Wickedness leads to division and sorrow.

Sadly, the Zion society described in 4 Nephi (see also Moses 7:18) eventually unraveled. As you read 4 Nephi 1:19–49, look for the attitudes and behaviors that caused this society to fall apart. Do you see any signs of these attitudes or behaviors in yourself?

See also "Chapter 18: Beware of Pride," *Teachings of Presidents of the Church: Ezra Taft Benson* (2014), 229–40.

Ideas for Family Scripture Study and Family Home Evening

As you read the scriptures with your family, the Spirit can help you know what principles to emphasize and discuss in order to meet the needs of your family. Here are some ideas.

3 Nephi 27:13–21. These verses can help family members better understand what the Savior meant when He referred to "my gospel." After reading and discussing these verses, you could ask each family member to summarize what the gospel is in one sentence.

3 Nephi 27:23–26. How are we doing at recording the things we have "seen and heard"—individually or as a family? Why is it important to keep a record of spiritual things?

3 Nephi 27:30–31. To help family members understand the joy the Savior described in these verses, you could play a game in which family members hide and another family member tries to find them. This could lead to a conversation about why it's important to find every family member so that "none of them are lost." How can we help our family members stay strong in the gospel or return if they have left?

3 Nephi 28:17–18, 36–40. What can we learn from Mormon's example when he did not understand everything about the change that happened to the three Nephite disciples? What can we do when we don't understand everything about a gospel principle? President Dieter F. Uchtdorf taught: "God cares about you. He will listen, and He will answer your personal questions. The answers to your prayers will come in His own way and in His own time, and therefore, you need to learn to listen to His voice" ("Receiving a Testimony of Light and Truth," *Ensign* or *Liahona,* Nov. 2014, 21).

4 Nephi 1:15. To reduce contention in your home, perhaps family members could set a goal to be more loving to each other this week. After the week is over, review your progress together and discuss how showing greater love has affected your family.

For more ideas for teaching children, see this week's outline in *Come, Follow Me—For Primary.*

Improving Personal Study

Seek revelation daily. Revelation often comes "line upon line" (2 Nephi 28:30). As you ponder the verses you are studying, ideas and impressions may come to you throughout the day. Don't think of gospel study as something you "make time for" but as something you are always doing (see *Teaching in the Savior's Way,* 12).

Christ with Three Nephite Disciples, by Gary L. Kapp

Mormon Abridging the Plates, by Tom Lovell

Mormon 1–6

"I WOULD THAT I COULD PERSUADE ALL . . . TO REPENT"

As you read Mormon 1–6, ponder what you learn from Mormon's example. Record what you feel inspired to do.

RECORD YOUR IMPRESSIONS_____

_____

_____

Mormon spared us the "full account" of the "awful scene" of wickedness and bloodshed that he saw among the Nephites (Mormon 2:18; 5:8). But what he did record in Mormon 1–6 is enough to remind us how far righteous people can fall. Amid such pervasive wickedness, no one could blame Mormon for becoming weary and even discouraged. Yet through all that he saw and experienced, he never lost his sense of God's great mercy and his conviction that repentance is the way to receive it. And although

Mormon's own people rejected his pleading invitations to repent, he knew that he had a larger audience to persuade. "Behold," he declared, "I write unto all the ends of the earth." In other words, he wrote to *you* (see Mormon 3:17–20). And his message to you, today, is the same message that could have saved the Nephites in their day: "Believe the gospel of Jesus Christ. . . . Repent and prepare to stand before the judgment-seat of Christ" (Mormon 3:21–22).

Ideas for Personal Scripture Study

MORMON 1

I can live righteously despite the wickedness around me.

Beginning in the first chapter of Mormon, you will notice major differences between Mormon and the people around him. As you read Mormon 1, consider contrasting the qualities and desires of Mormon with those of his people. Note the consequences that came to him and them (you'll find one example in verses 14–15). What do you learn that inspires you to live righteously in a wicked world?

As you read Mormon 2–6, continue to look for how Mormon demonstrated his faith in Heavenly Father and Jesus Christ despite the evil influences around him.

Battle, by Jorge Cocco

MORMON 2:10–15

Godly sorrow leads to true and lasting change.

When Mormon saw his people's sorrow, he hoped they would repent. But "their sorrowing was not unto repentance" (Mormon 2:13)—it was not the kind of godly sorrow that leads to real change (see 2 Corinthians 7:8–11). Instead, the Nephites felt worldly sorrow (see Mormon 2:10–11). To understand the difference between godly sorrow and worldly sorrow, consider making a chart where you can record what you learn from Mormon 2:10–15 about these two types of sorrow. Your chart might look something like this:

Godly sorrow	Worldly sorrow
Comes to Jesus (verse 14)	Curses God (verse 14)

As you reflect on what you learn, consider how it can influence your efforts to overcome sin and become more like Heavenly Father and the Savior.

See also Dieter F. Uchtdorf, "You Can Do It Now!" *Ensign* or *Liahona,* Nov. 2013, 55–57.

MORMON 3:3, 9

I should always acknowledge God's hand in my life.

Mormon recorded a weakness he saw in the Nephites: they failed to acknowledge the ways the Lord had blessed them. President Henry B. Eyring urged us "to find ways to recognize and remember God's kindness. . . . Pray and ponder, asking the questions: Did God send a message that was just for me? Did I see His hand in my life or the lives of my children? . . . I testify that He loves us and blesses us, more than most of us have yet recognized" ("O Remember, Remember," *Ensign* or *Liahona,* Nov. 2007, 67, 69).

As you read Mormon 3:3, 9, you might ponder how you are acknowledging God's influence in your life. What blessings come when you acknowledge His influence? What are the consequences of not acknowledging Him? (see Mormon 2:26).

MORMON 5:8–24; 6:16–22

Jesus Christ stands with open arms to receive me.

The Nephites rejected Mormon's teachings, but he had hope that his record would influence you. As you read Mormon 5:8–24 and 6:16–22, what do you learn about the consequences of sin? What do you learn from these passages about Heavenly Father's and Jesus's feelings toward you, even when you sin? How have you felt Jesus Christ reaching out to you with open arms? What do you feel inspired to do as a result?

Ideas for Family Scripture Study and Family Home Evening

As you read the scriptures with your family, the Spirit can help you know what principles to emphasize and discuss in order to meet the needs of your family. Here are some ideas.

Mormon 1:2. What does it mean to be "quick to observe"? You can find insights in Elder David A. Bednar's article "Quick to Observe" (*Ensign,* Dec. 2006, 30–36). How was the gift of being quick to observe a blessing to Mormon? How can it be a blessing to us?

Mormon 1:1–6, 15; 2:1–2. Do the children in your family understand that they can develop great spiritual qualities and power even though they are young? Mormon's example could help them. Consider making a timeline of Mormon's childhood and youth, using the ages and events given in Mormon 1:1–6, 15 and 2:1–2. As you discuss Mormon's qualities and experiences, point out qualities your children have that inspire you and others around them.

Mormon 2:18–19. What words did Mormon use to describe the world he lived in? How did he maintain hope despite the wickedness around him? How can our family do the same?

Mormon 3:12. How did Mormon feel about the people around him, even though they were wicked? What can we do to develop the kind of love he had?

Mormon 5:2. Why might we hesitate to call upon Heavenly Father when we are struggling? What can we do to rely on Heavenly Father more?

Mormon 5:16–18. To help your family visualize what it means to be "driven about as chaff before the wind" (verse 16), tear a piece of paper into small pieces and let family members blow them around. Explain to them that chaff is a husk that comes off a seed, and it is light enough to be blown around. How is being "without Christ and God in the world" (verse 16) like being chaff in the wind?

For more ideas for teaching children, see this week's outline in *Come, Follow Me—For Primary.*

Improving Our Teaching

Teach clear and simple doctrine.

The Lord's gospel is beautiful in its simplicity (see D&C 133:57). Rather than trying to entertain your family with extravagant lessons, make sure that what you teach is centered on pure and simple doctrine.

Mormon's Miraculous Book, by Joseph Brickey

Moroni Writing on Gold Plates, by Dale Kilbourn

Mormon 7–9

"I SPEAK UNTO YOU AS IF YE WERE PRESENT"

Mormon and Moroni had faith that their record would inspire those living in the latter days. As you read Mormon 7–9, write the impressions that come to you about how you can apply what you are learning.

RECORD YOUR IMPRESSIONS

Mormon and Moroni knew what it felt like to be alone in a wicked world. For Moroni the loneliness must have been especially severe after his father died in battle and the Nephites were destroyed. "I even remain alone," he wrote. "I have not friends nor whither to go" (Mormon 8:3, 5). Things may have seemed hopeless, but Moroni found hope in his testimony of the Savior and his knowledge that "the eternal purposes of the Lord shall roll on" (Mormon 8:22). And Moroni knew that a key role in those eternal purposes would be played by the Book of Mormon—the record he was now diligently completing, the record that would one day "shine forth out of darkness" and bring many people "to the knowledge of Christ" (Mormon 8:16; 9:36). Moroni's faith in these promises made it possible for him to declare to the future readers of this book, "I speak unto you as if ye were present" and "I know that ye shall have my words" (Mormon 8:35; 9:30). Now we *do* have his words, and the Lord's work *is* rolling forth, in part because Mormon and Moroni stayed true to their mission, even when they were alone.

Ideas for Personal Scripture Study

MORMON 7

I must believe in Jesus Christ and "lay hold" upon His gospel.

Mormon's last recorded words, found in Mormon 7, are addressed to the latter-day descendants of the Lamanites, but they contain truths that are for all of us. What does Mormon's message teach you about Jesus Christ and His gospel? Why might Mormon have chosen this message to conclude his writings?

MORMON 7:8–10; 8:12–22; 9:31–37

The Book of Mormon is of great worth.

President Russell M. Nelson asked: "If you were offered diamonds or rubies *or* the Book of Mormon, which would you choose? Honestly, which *is* of greater worth to you?" ("The Book of Mormon: What Would Your Life Be Like without It?" *Ensign* or *Liahona,* Nov. 2017, 61).

Mormon and Moroni knew the record they were keeping would be of great worth in our day, so they made great sacrifices to prepare and protect it. As you read Mormon 7:8–10; 8:12–22; and 9:31–37, consider why the record is so valuable in our day. You may find additional insights in 1 Nephi 13:38–41; 2 Nephi 3:11–12; and Doctrine and Covenants 33:16; 42:12–13. What experiences have helped you know that the Book of Mormon is of great worth?

The writings of Book of Mormon prophets apply to us.

MORMON 8:26–41; 9:1–30

The Book of Mormon was written for our day.

Jesus Christ showed Moroni what would be happening when the Book of Mormon came forth (see Mormon 8:34–35), and what Moroni saw led him to give bold warnings for our day. As you read Mormon 8:26–41 and 9:1–30, ponder whether there are any signs of these attitudes and actions in your life. What could you do differently?

For example, Mormon 9:1–30 contains Moroni's message in response to the widespread lack of belief in Jesus Christ he foresaw in our day. Consider recording what you learn from his words about the following:

- The consequences of not believing in Christ (verses 1–6, 26)

- The importance of believing in a God of revelation and miracles (verses 7–20)

- Moroni's counsel for us (verses 21–30)

What do you learn from Moroni that can help you bring others closer to Heavenly Father and Jesus Christ?

Ideas for Family Scripture Study and Family Home Evening

As you read the scriptures with your family, the Spirit can help you know what principles to emphasize and discuss in order to meet the needs of your family. Here are some ideas.

Mormon 7:5–7, 10; 9:11–14. What do these verses teach us about Heavenly Father's plan and why we need a Savior?

Mormon 7:8–10. What have we learned in our study of the Book of Mormon this year that has helped strengthen our belief in the Bible? To begin a discussion, you could read together some scriptures from the Book of Mormon and the Bible that teach similar truths, such as Alma 7:11–13 and Isaiah 53:3–5 or 3 Nephi 15:16–24 and John 10:16.

Mormon 8:1–9. How might it have felt to be alone like Moroni was? What impresses us about the work he accomplished?

Mormon 8:12, 17–21; 9:31. Consider reading these verses as a family and then reading the following statement by Elder Jeffrey R. Holland: "Except in the case of His only perfect Begotten Son, imperfect people are all God has ever had to work with.

. . . When you see imperfection, remember that the limitation is *not* in the divinity of the work" ("Lord, I Believe," *Ensign* or *Liahona,* May 2013, 94). Why is it dangerous to focus on imperfections in others, including those who wrote the Book of Mormon?

Mormon 8:36–38. What does it mean to take the name of Jesus Christ upon us? Why might someone be ashamed to take upon himself or herself the name of Jesus Christ? How can we be bold in our testimonies of the Savior?

Mormon 9:16–24. Certain ingredients are needed to make a science experiment or recipe work successfully. Consider doing an experiment or making a favorite recipe as a family before reading Mormon 9:16–24. As you read the verses (especially verses 20–21), look for the necessary "ingredients" that make miracles possible. What miracles can we see in the world around us and in our family?

For more ideas for teaching children, see this week's outline in *Come, Follow Me—For Primary.*

Improving Personal Study

Refer to official Church resources. If you have gospel questions, the best sources for answers are prayer, the scriptures, the words of living prophets, and other official Church publications (see *Teaching in the Savior's Way,* 17–18, 23–24).

Mormon Abridging the Plates, by Jon McNaughton

The Jaredites Leaving Babel, by Albin Veselka

Ether 1–5

"REND THAT VEIL OF UNBELIEF"

The book of Ether is the record of the Jaredites, who arrived in the promised land centuries before the Nephites. God inspired Moroni to include Ether's record in the Book of Mormon because of its relevance to our day. How do you feel it is relevant to your life?

RECORD YOUR IMPRESSIONS _____

_____

_____

While it is true that God's ways are higher than ours, and we should always submit to His will, He also encourages us to think and act for ourselves. That's one lesson Jared and his brother learned. For example, the idea of traveling to a new land that was "choice above all the earth" seemed to start in Jared's mind, and the Lord "had compassion" and promised to grant the request, saying, "Thus I will do unto thee because this long time ye have cried unto me" (see Ether 1:38–43). And when the brother of Jared realized how dark it was inside the barges that would carry them to their promised land, the Lord invited him to suggest a solution, asking a question that *we* usually ask *Him:* "What will ye that I should do?" (Ether 2:23). The message seems to be that we shouldn't expect God to command us in all things. We can share with Him our own thoughts and ideas, and He will listen and give His confirmation or else counsel us otherwise. Sometimes the only thing separating us from the blessings we seek is our own "veil of unbelief," and if we can "rend that veil" (Ether 4:15), we may be surprised by what the Lord is willing to do for us.

Ideas for Personal Scripture Study

ETHER 1:33–43

As I cry unto the Lord, He will have compassion on me.

Ether 1:33–43 tells of three prayers of the brother of Jared. What do you learn from the Lord's response to each of these prayers? Think about a time when you have experienced the Lord's compassion as you cried unto Him in prayer. You may want to record this experience and share it with someone who may need to hear your testimony.

ETHER 2; 3:1–6; 4:7–15

I can receive revelation for my life.

President Russell M. Nelson said: "I plead with you to increase your spiritual capacity to receive revelation. . . . Choose to do the spiritual work required to enjoy the gift of the Holy Ghost and hear the voice of the Spirit more frequently and more clearly" ("Revelation for the Church, Revelation for Our Lives," *Ensign* or *Liahona,* May 2018, 96).

As you study Ether 2; 3:1–6; and 4:7–15, what truths do you find that help you understand how to seek personal revelation? You could mark in one color the questions or concerns the brother of Jared had and what he did about them, and in another color you could mark how the Lord helped him and made His will known. What impresses you about the way the brother of Jared conversed with the Lord, and what do you learn from this about how to increase the flow of revelation in your life?

ETHER 2:16–25

The Lord will prepare me to cross my "great deep."

To get to the promised land, the Jaredites faced a major obstacle: crossing the "great deep" (Ether 2:25). The phrase "great deep" can be a fitting way to describe what our trials and challenges sometimes feel like. And sometimes, as was the case for the Jaredites, crossing our own "great deep" is the only way to fulfill God's will for us. Do you see similarities to your life in Ether 2:16–25? How has the Lord prepared you for your challenges? What might He be asking you to do now to prepare for what He needs you to do in the future?

ETHER 3

I am created in God's image.

On Mount Shelem, the brother of Jared learned a lot about God and about himself. What do you learn from Ether 3 about the spiritual and physical nature of God? How do these truths help you understand your divine identity and potential?

We are all children of God.

ETHER 3:6–16

Was the brother of Jared the first person to see the Lord?

God had shown Himself to other prophets before the brother of Jared (for example, see Moses 7:4, 59), so why did the Lord say to him, "Never have I showed myself unto man"? (Ether 3:15). Elder Jeffrey R.

Holland offered this possible explanation: "Christ was saying to the brother of Jared, 'Never have I showed myself unto man *in this manner, without my volition, driven solely by the faith of the beholder*'" (*Christ and the New Covenant* [1997], 23).

Ideas for Family Scripture Study and Family Home Evening

As you read the scriptures with your family, the Spirit can help you know what principles to emphasize and discuss in order to meet the needs of your family. Here are some ideas.

Ether 1:34–37. What do we learn from these verses about praying for others? What other truths about prayer do these verses illustrate?

Ether 2:16–3:6. What does the brother of Jared's example teach us about how to find answers to our problems and questions? Maybe family members could share experiences when they sought and received answers from the Lord.

Ether 4:11–12. After reading these verses, family members could write down some everyday things that influence your family (such as movies, songs, games, or people) on slips of paper and place them in a bowl. Then they could take turns picking one and discussing whether it "persuadeth [them] to do good" (Ether 4:12). What changes does your family feel inspired to make?

Ether 5. You could hide an object or a treat in a box and invite a family member to look inside and give the rest of the family clues to help them guess what it is. As you read Ether 5 together, discuss why it is important that the Lord uses witnesses in His work. How can we share our witness of the Book of Mormon with others?

For more ideas for teaching children, see this week's outline in *Come, Follow Me—For Primary.*

Improving Our Teaching

Be ready always. "Informal teaching moments pass quickly, so it is important to take advantage of them when they arise. . . . For example, a teenager with a difficult decision to make may be ready to learn about how to receive personal revelation" (*Teaching in the Savior's Way,* 16).

Sawest Thou More Than This? by Marcus Alan Vincent

I Will Bring You up Again out of the Depths, by Jonathan Arthur Clarke

NOVEMBER 16–22

Ether 6–11

"THAT EVIL MAY BE DONE AWAY"

Speaking of the Jaredite record, Mormon commented that "it is expedient that all people should know the things which are written in this account" (Mosiah 28:19). Keep this in mind as you read Ether 6–11. Why are these things expedient—or beneficial—to you and your loved ones?

RECORD YOUR IMPRESSIONS _____

_____

_____

Hundreds of years after the Jaredites were destroyed, the Nephites discovered the ruins of their ancient civilization. Among these ruins was a mysterious record—plates of "pure gold" that were "filled with engravings" (Mosiah 8:9). The Nephite king, Limhi, could sense that this record was important: "Doubtless a great mystery is contained within these plates," he said (Mosiah 8:19). Today you have an abridgment of this record, translated into your language, and it's called the book of Ether. It comes from the same record that the Nephites "were desirous beyond measure" to read, and when they

did, "they were filled with sorrow; nevertheless it gave them much knowledge, in the which they did rejoice" (Mosiah 28:12, 18). As you read about the rise and the tragic fall of the Jaredites, you'll find many sorrowful moments. But don't overlook the joy of learning lessons from this history. After all, as Moroni wrote, "it is wisdom in God that these things should be shown unto you" (Ether 8:23), for if we can learn from the failures and the successes of the Jaredites, "evil may be done away, and . . . the time may come that Satan may have no power upon the hearts of the children of men" (Ether 8:26).

Ideas for Personal Scripture Study

ETHER 6:1–12

The Lord will lead me toward my promised land.

You may find spiritual insights if you compare the Jaredites' voyage across the ocean to your journey through mortality. For example, what has the Lord provided that lights your way like the stones in the Jaredites' barges? What might the barges represent, or the winds that "blow towards the promised land"? (Ether 6:8). What do you learn from the actions of the Jaredites before, during, and after the voyage? How is the Lord leading you toward your promised land?

Minerva K. Teichert (1888–1976), *Journey of the Jaredites across Asia,* 1935, oil on linen on masonite, 35 x 48 inches. Brigham Young University Museum of Art.

ETHER 6:5–18, 30; 9:28–35; 10:1–2

The Lord blesses me when I am humble.

Although pride and wickedness seem to dominate Jaredite history, there are also examples of humility in these chapters—especially in Ether 6:5–18, 30; 9:28–35; and 10:1–2. Pondering the following questions could help you learn from these examples: Why did these Jaredites humble themselves in these situations?

What did they do to show their humility? How were they blessed as a result? Notice that in some cases, the people were compelled by their circumstances to be humble. Consider what you can do to willingly "walk humbly before the Lord" (Ether 6:17) rather than be compelled to be humble (see Mosiah 4:11–12; Alma 32:14–18).

See also "Humility," Gospel Topics, topics.ChurchofJesusChrist.org.

ETHER 7–11

Righteous leaders bless the people they lead.

Chapters 7–11 of Ether cover at least 28 generations. Although not much detail can be given in such little space, a pattern quickly emerges: righteous leadership leads to blessings and prosperity, while wicked leadership leads to captivity and destruction.

Below are just a few of the kings mentioned in these chapters. Read the associated verses, and see what you can learn from their examples—positive and negative—about leadership. As you do, think about opportunities you might have to lead or influence others in your home, your community, your Church calling, and so on.

Orihah—Ether 6:30–7:1

Shule—Ether 7:23–27

Jared—Ether 8:1–7, 11–15

Emer and Coriantum—Ether 9:21–23

Heth—Ether 9:26–30

Shez—Ether 10:1–2

Riplakish—Ether 10:5–8

Morianton—Ether 10:10–11

Lib—Ether 10:19–28

Ethem—Ether 11:11–13

ETHER 8:7–26

What is a secret combination?

When two or more people conspire to keep their wicked acts secret, they are involved in a secret combination. They are often motivated by the desire for power or riches. In addition to the secret combination described in Ether 8:7–18, other examples can be found in Helaman 1:9–12; 2:2–11; 6:16–30; and Moses 5:29–33. In Ether 8:18–26, Moroni describes the consequences of secret combinations (see also Ether 9:4–12) and warns us not to support them.

Ideas for Family Scripture Study and Family Home Evening

As you read the scriptures with your family, the Spirit can help you know what principles to emphasize and discuss in order to meet the needs of your family. Here are some ideas.

Ether 6:2–12. Would your family enjoy acting out the Jaredites' voyage to the promised land? Maybe you could use a dark room as a barge and flashlights to represent the shining stones. You could talk about how the Jaredites showed their faith in the Lord by getting in the barges, despite knowing that they would be "buried in the depths of the sea" (Ether 6:6). After reading verse 9, family members could share favorite hymns of praise and sing them together. How can our homes be compared to the Jaredites' barges? What is the promised land the Lord is leading our family toward?

Ether 6:22–23. Throughout this week, your family could watch for how the brother of Jared's prophetic warning about captivity was fulfilled. What warnings have our Church leaders given us? In what ways could dismissing their counsel lead to captivity?

Ether 8:23–26. According to these verses, why was Moroni commanded to write "these things" about secret combinations? (Ether 8:23). What have we learned from the book of Ether that can help us obtain the blessings described in verse 26?

Ether 9:11. How do our desires affect our choices? What can we do as a family to ensure that we desire the things of God?

Ether 11:8. To learn more about the Lord's mercy to those who repent, you could read Mosiah 26:29–30; 29:18–20; Alma 34:14–16; or Moroni 6:8. Perhaps family members could share examples of God's mercy from the scriptures or from their own lives.

For more ideas for teaching children, see this week's outline in *Come, Follow Me—For Primary.*

Improving Personal Study

Act on what you learn. Gospel learning includes more than reading and pondering. We often learn the most by acting on the truths in the scriptures (see John 7:17). What will you do to apply what you read in Ether 6–11?

Jaredite Barges, by Gary Ernest Smith

Ether Hiding in the Cavity of a Rock, by Gary Ernest Smith

Ether 12–15

"BY FAITH ALL THINGS ARE FULFILLED"

Recording impressions can invite further revelation and strengthen your testimony. It also helps you remember your impressions and share them with others in the future.

RECORD YOUR IMPRESSIONS _____

Ether's prophecies to the Jaredites were "great and marvelous" (Ether 12:5). He "told them of all things, from the beginning of man" (Ether 13:2). He foresaw "the days of Christ" and the latter-day New Jerusalem (Ether 13:4). And he spoke of "hope for a better world, yea, even a place at the right hand of God" (Ether 12:4). But the Jaredites rejected his words, for the same reason people often reject the prophecies of God's servants today—"because they [see] them not" (Ether 12:5). It takes faith to believe in promises or warnings about things we can't see, just as it took faith for Ether to prophesy of "great and marvelous things" to an unbelieving people. It took faith for Moroni to trust that the Lord could take his "weakness in writing" and turn it into strength (see Ether 12:23–27). It's this kind of faith that makes us "sure and steadfast, always abounding in good works, being led to glorify God" (Ether 12:4). And it's this kind of faith by which "all things are fulfilled" (Ether 12:3).

Ideas for Personal Scripture Study

ETHER 12

Faith in Jesus Christ can lead to mighty miracles.

Many people today, like the Jaredites in Ether's day, want to see evidence before they will believe in God and His power. However, Moroni taught that "faith is things which are hoped for and not seen" and that you "receive no witness until after the trial of your faith" (Ether 12:6).

Note each time you find the word "faith" in Ether 12, and record what you learn about faith. Look for answers to questions like these: What is faith? What are the fruits of a faith-filled life? You could also record your thoughts about witnesses you have gained "after the trial of your faith" (Ether 12:6).

See also Hebrews 11; Alma 32.

ETHER 12:1–9, 28, 32

Jesus Christ gives us "a more excellent hope."

In addition to profound insights about faith, Ether 12 also has a lot to say about hope—maybe you could note each time the word "hope" appears. What does hope mean to you? What were the reasons that Ether had to "hope for a better world"? (see Ether 12:2–5). How has the gospel of Jesus Christ given you "a more excellent hope"? (Ether 12:32).

See also Moroni 7:40–41; Dieter F. Uchtdorf, "The Infinite Power of Hope," *Ensign* or *Liahona,* Nov. 2008, 21–24; *Preach My Gospel,* 117.

ETHER 12:23–29

Jesus Christ can make weak things strong.

When we read Moroni's powerful writings, it's easy to forget that he worried about his "weakness in writing" and feared that people would mock his words (see Ether 12:23–25). But God promised that He would "make weak things become strong" for the humble (verse 27), and the spiritual power in Moroni's writings is convincing evidence that the Lord fulfilled this promise.

After reading Ether 12:23–29, ponder times when God has helped you recognize your weaknesses and made you strong in spite of them. Maybe this is also a good time to think about weaknesses you are currently struggling with. What do you feel you need to do to humble yourself before the Lord and show faith in Him in order to receive His promise to "make weak things become strong"? (Ether 12:27).

As you ponder these verses, the following insight from Elder Neal A. Maxwell may be helpful: "When we read in the scriptures of man's 'weakness,' this term includes the . . . weakness inherent in the general human condition in which the flesh has an incessant impact upon the spirit (see Ether 12:28–29). Weakness likewise includes, however, our specific, individual weaknesses, which we are expected to overcome (see Doctrine and Covenants 66:3; Jacob 4:7)" (*Lord, Increase Our Faith* [1994], 84).

See also "Grace," Gospel Topics, topics.ChurchofJesusChrist.org.

ETHER 13:13–22; 14–15

Rejecting the prophets brings spiritual danger.

Being king of the Jaredites was, historically, a dangerous position. This was especially true for Coriantumr, as many "mighty men . . . sought to destroy him" (Ether 13:15–16). In Ether 13:15–22, notice what Coriantumr did to protect himself and what the prophet Ether counseled him to do instead. As you read the rest of the book of Ether, ponder the consequences of rejecting the prophets. What happens to people when "the Spirit of the Lord [ceases] striving with them"? (Ether 15:19).

Ideas for Family Scripture Study and Family Home Evening

As you read the scriptures with your family, the Spirit can help you know what principles to emphasize and discuss in order to meet the needs of your family. Here are some ideas.

Ether 12:7–22. As you read these verses together, you might review some inspiring examples of faith you have read about in the Book of Mormon. This could lead to a discussion about examples of faith in your family history or your own lives—consider recording these experiences if you haven't already.

Ether 12:27. Why does the Lord give us weakness? What is our part in making "weak things become strong"? What is the Savior's part?

Ether 12:41. Is there a fun way you could teach your children to "seek . . . Jesus"? One way might be to hide a picture of Jesus and invite your family members to "seek" and find the picture. How do we seek Jesus, and how are we blessed when we find Him?

Ether 13:13–14; 15:19, 33–34. It might be interesting for your family members to compare the experience of Ether with the experiences of Mormon and Moroni (see Mormon 6; 8:1–10). How are they similar? How was the Nephites' path to destruction similar to the Jaredites' path? (compare Ether 15:19 with Moroni 8:28). What truths do we learn that can help us avoid what happened to them?

For more ideas for teaching children, see this week's outline in *Come, Follow Me—For Primary.*

Improving Our Teaching

Encourage questions. Children are naturally curious. Sometimes you might see their questions as a distraction from what you're trying to teach. Instead, see questions as opportunities. They are an indication that children are ready to learn—they give you insight into your children's concerns and how they feel about what they're learning (see *Teaching in the Savior's Way,* 25–26).

Marvelous Were the Prophecies of Ether, by Walter Rane

Minerva K. Teichert (1888–1976), *Alma Baptizes in the Waters of Mormon*, 1949–1951, oil on masonite, 35⅞ x 48 inches. Brigham Young University Museum of Art, 1969.

NOVEMBER 30–DECEMBER 6

Moroni 1–6

"TO KEEP THEM IN THE RIGHT WAY"

Moroni recorded what he hoped would "be of worth . . . in some future day" (Moroni 1:4). What do you find in Moroni 1–6 that is of worth to you? Record what you discover, and consider sharing it with someone who also might find it valuable.

RECORD YOUR IMPRESSIONS _____

_____

_____

After finishing his father's record of the Nephites and abridging the record of the Jaredites, Moroni thought at first that his record-keeping work was done (see Moroni 1:1). What more was there to say about two nations that were utterly destroyed? But Moroni had seen our times (see Mormon 8:35), and he was inspired to "write a few more things, that perhaps they may be of worth . . . in some future day" (Moroni 1:4). He knew that widespread apostasy was coming, bringing with it confusion about priesthood ordinances and religion in general. This may be why he gave clarifying details about the sacrament, baptism, conferring the gift of the Holy Ghost, and the blessings of gathering with fellow believers to "keep [each other] in the right way, . . . relying alone upon the merits of Christ, who was the author and the finisher of [our] faith" (Moroni 6:4). Precious insights like these give us reason to be thankful that the Lord preserved Moroni's life so he could "write a few more things" (Moroni 1:4).

Ideas for Personal Scripture Study

MORONI 1

Disciples of Jesus Christ remain faithful despite opposition.

For some people, it's easier to be faithful in times of ease and comfort. But as disciples of Jesus Christ, we must remain faithful even when we face trials and opposition. As you read Moroni 1, what inspires you about Moroni's faithfulness to the Lord and to his calling? How can you follow his example?

MORONI 2–6

Priesthood ordinances must be administered as the Lord commands.

During His mortal ministry, the Savior received and administered sacred ordinances, such as baptism (see Matthew 3:13–17; Joseph Smith Translation, John 4:1–3 [in the Bible appendix]), priesthood ordination (see Mark 3:13–19), and the sacrament (see Matthew 26:26–28). However, because of the Great Apostasy, many people today are confused about how ordinances must be performed—and even whether they are needed at all. In Moroni 2–6, Moroni provided important details about certain priesthood ordinances that can help clear up some of that confusion. What impressions come as you learn about the ordinances in these chapters? The following are some questions you might ask to help you learn:

Confirmation (Moroni 2; 6:4). What do the Savior's instructions in Moroni 2:2 teach you about the ordinance of confirmation? What do you think it means to be "wrought upon and cleansed by the power of the Holy Ghost"? (Moroni 6:4).

Priesthood ordination (Moroni 3). What do you find in this chapter that could help someone prepare

to be ordained to the priesthood? What do you find that would help someone perform an ordination?

The sacrament (Moroni 4–5; 6:6). Note the promises in the sacrament prayers (see Moroni 4:3; 5:2), and ponder what you are doing to keep your promises. What can you do to invite the influence of the Spirit more powerfully as you participate in the sacrament?

Baptism (Moroni 6:1–3). What can you do to continue to meet the qualifications for baptism given in these verses, even after you are baptized? What do these verses suggest to you about what it means to be a member of the Church of Jesus Christ?

Based on what you have learned, how will you change the ways you think about, participate in, or prepare others for these ordinances? Why is it important that these ordinances be "administered . . . according to the commandments of Christ"? (Moroni 4:1).

See also "Ordinances," Gospel Topics, topics.ChurchofJesusChrist.org.

Jesus taught how ordinances should be performed.

MORONI 6:4–9

Disciples of Jesus Christ look after the welfare of each other's souls.

While it's true that we all "work out [our] own salvation" (Mormon 9:27), Moroni also taught that "meet[ing] together oft" with fellow believers can help keep us "in the right way" (Moroni 6:4–5). As you read Moroni 6:4–9, ponder the blessings that come from being "numbered among the people of the church of Christ" (Moroni 6:4). How could you help make the experiences you and others have at church more like the one Moroni describes, whether you are a leader or a participant?

Ideas for Family Scripture Study and Family Home Evening

As you read the scriptures with your family, the Spirit can help you know what principles to emphasize and discuss in order to meet the needs of your family. Here are some ideas.

Moroni 1; Moroni 6:3. What does it mean to "deny the Christ"? (Moroni 1:2–3). How can we show our "determination to serve him to the end"? (Moroni 6:3). Share examples of people you know who have this determination to serve Him.

Moroni 4:3; Moroni 5:2. Reading the sacrament prayers as a family could lead to a discussion about treating the sacrament with more reverence. Perhaps family members could discuss phrases from these prayers that are especially meaningful to them. They could also record their thoughts about these phrases or draw a picture that helps them think about the Savior. They could bring what they wrote or drew to sacrament meeting to help them focus their thoughts on Him. Tell your family how you feel about the sacrament and the Savior's sacrifice.

Moroni 6:1–4. What does it mean to have a "broken heart and a contrite spirit"? (Moroni 6:2). How does this help us prepare for baptism? How might it help us after we are baptized?

Moroni 6:4–9. According to these verses, what are some of the blessings that come from being "numbered among the people of the church of Christ"? (Moroni 6:4). Why do we need the Church?

Moroni 6:8. What does this verse teach about repentance? What does it mean to seek forgiveness with "real intent"? (Moroni 6:8). Consider singing a song about forgiveness, such as "Help Me, Dear Father" (*Children's Songbook,* 99).

For more ideas for teaching children, see this week's outline in *Come, Follow Me—For Primary.*

Improving Personal Study

Find evidence of God's love. President M. Russell Ballard taught, "[The] gospel is a gospel of love—love for God and love for one another" ("God's Love for His Children," *Ensign,* May 1988, 59). As you read the scriptures, consider noting or marking evidences of God's love for you and all of His children.

Moroni in the Cave, by Jorge Cocco

Minerva K. Teichert (1888–1976), Moroni: The Lost Nephite, 1949–1951, oil on masonite, 34¾ x 47 inches. Brigham Young University Museum of Art, 1969

Moroni 7–9

"MAY CHRIST LIFT THEE UP"

As you study Moroni 7–9, listen to the promptings of the Holy Ghost, and record His messages to you. He can teach you both what you need to know and what you need to do.

RECORD YOUR IMPRESSIONS

Before Moroni concluded the record we know today as the Book of Mormon with his own final words, he shared three messages from his father, Mormon: an address to "the peaceable followers of Christ" (Moroni 7:3) and two letters that Mormon had written to Moroni. Perhaps Moroni included these messages in the Book of Mormon because he foresaw similarities between the perils of his day and ours. When these words were written, the Nephite people as a whole were tumbling headlong into apostasy. Many of them had "lost their love, one towards another" and delighted in "everything save that which is good" (Moroni 9:5, 19). And yet Mormon still found cause for hope—teaching us that hope does not mean ignoring or being naive about the world's problems; it means having faith in Heavenly Father and Jesus Christ, whose power is greater and more everlasting than those problems. It means "lay[ing] hold upon every good thing" (Moroni 7:19). It means letting the Atonement of Jesus Christ "and the hope of his glory and of eternal life, rest in your mind" (Moroni 9:25). And until the glorious day of Christ's Second Coming, it means never ceasing the "labor [we have] to perform . . . [to] conquer the enemy of all righteousness" (Moroni 9:6).

Ideas for Personal Scripture Study

The light of Christ helps me judge between good and evil.

Today's world is full of influential messages; how can we tell which are right and which are wrong? Mormon's words in Moroni 7 give us several principles we can use to avoid "judg[ing] wrongfully" (Moroni 7:18). As you study Moroni 7:12–20, look for truths that can help you know what will bring you closer to God and what won't. You might use these truths to help you evaluate the messages you encounter and the experiences you have this week and determine whether or not they invite and entice you to do good (see Moroni 7:13).

See also "Judging Others," Gospel Topics, topics.ChurchofJesusChrist.org; Bible Dictionary, "Light of Christ."

Through faith in Christ, I can "lay hold upon every good thing."

After teaching about how to distinguish between good and evil, Mormon asked a question that seems relevant today: "How is it possible [to] lay hold upon every good thing?"—especially when the adversary's temptations are so enticing (Moroni 7:20). Mormon's answer can be found throughout the rest of chapter 7. As you read verses 20–48, look for truths that help you recognize "every good thing" you have because of Jesus Christ. How does having faith in Him help you seek out things that are good? How can you "lay hold" on more good things?

See also Articles of Faith 1:13.

"Charity is the pure love of Christ."

President Dallin H. Oaks observed: "The reason charity never fails and the reason charity is greater than even the most significant acts of goodness . . . is that charity, 'the pure love of Christ' (Moro. 7:47), is not an *act* but a *condition* or state of being. . . . Charity is something one becomes" ("The Challenge to Become," *Ensign,* Nov. 2000, 34). As you read Moroni 7:44–48, consider Mormon's description of charity, and listen for impressions from the Holy Ghost; He can help you find ways you could improve. Why do we need faith and hope to receive the gift of charity?

Can my chastity and virtue be taken from me?

Mormon's description of the horrible sins of the Nephites have led some to mistakenly conclude that victims of sexual assault or abuse have violated the law of chastity. However, Elder Richard G. Scott clarified that this is not the case. He taught, "I solemnly testify that when another's acts of violence, perversion, or incest hurt you terribly, against your will, you are not responsible and you must not feel guilty" ("Healing the Tragic Scars of Abuse," *Ensign,* May 1992, 32).

I can have hope in Christ regardless of my circumstances.

After describing the wickedness he had seen, Mormon told his son not to grieve. What impresses you about Mormon's message of hope? What does it mean to you for Christ to "lift [you] up"? What attributes of Christ and principles of His gospel "rest in your mind" and give you hope? (Moroni 9:25).

See also Dieter F. Uchtdorf, "The Hope of God's Light," *Ensign* or *Liahona,* May 2013, 70, 75–77.

Ideas for Family Scripture Study and Family Home Evening

As you read the scriptures with your family, the Spirit can help you know what principles to emphasize and discuss in order to meet the needs of your family. Here are some ideas.

Moroni 7:5–11. According to Moroni 7:5–11, why is it important to do the right things for the right reasons? How can we know if we are praying and obeying God's commandments with "real intent"? (verse 6).

Moroni 7:12–19. How can Mormon's counsel help us make good choices about how we spend our time and who we spend it with? You could invite family members to search your home and "lay hold upon" (Moroni 7:19), or hold on to, things that invite them "to do good, and to love God, and to serve him" (Moroni 7:13). Praise them for the good things they find.

Moroni 7:29. After reading this verse, family members could talk about miracles they have witnessed or other ways they have seen God's hand in their lives.

Moroni 8:5–26. What did the Nephites who were baptizing little children misunderstand about the Atonement of Jesus Christ? What do we learn about the Atonement from Mormon's teachings?

Moroni 8:16–17. What does it mean to have "perfect love"? How does it help us overcome fear? How does it help us teach truth with boldness? How do we develop it?

For more ideas for teaching children, see this week's outline in *Come, Follow Me—For Primary.*

Improving Our Teaching

Use music to invite the Spirit and teach doctrine. "Music has boundless powers for moving [us] toward greater spirituality" ("First Presidency Preface," *Hymns,* x). A song about love, such as "Love One Another" (*Hymns,* no. 308), could enhance a family discussion about charity in Moroni 7:44–48.

Portrait of Christ the Savior, by Heinrich Hofmann

That Ye May Know, by Gary L. Kapp

Moroni 10

"COME UNTO CHRIST, AND BE PERFECTED IN HIM"

As you finish reading the Book of Mormon, consider seeking a renewed witness from the Holy Ghost that it is true. As you do, record the impressions you receive.

RECORD YOUR IMPRESSIONS

The Book of Mormon opens with Nephi's promise to show us that "the tender mercies of the Lord are over all those whom he hath chosen, because of their faith" (1 Nephi 1:20). The book closes with a similar message from Moroni as he prepared to "seal up" the records: he invited us to "remember how merciful the Lord hath been" (Moroni 10:2–3). Even if we think only of the many mercies recorded in the Book of Mormon, this gives us a lot to think about. What examples come to your mind? You might ponder the merciful way God led Lehi's family through the wilderness and across the great waters, the tender mercies He showed to Enos when his soul hungered

for forgiveness, or the mercy He showed to Alma, a bitter enemy of the Church who became one of its fearless defenders. Or your thoughts might turn to the mercy the resurrected Savior showed to the people when He healed their sick and blessed their little children. Perhaps most important, all of this can remind you of "how merciful the Lord hath been" to you, for one of the main purposes of the Book of Mormon is to invite each of us to receive God's mercy—an invitation expressed simply in Moroni's farewell words, "Come unto Christ, and be perfected in him" (Moroni 10:32).

Ideas for Personal Scripture Study

MORONI 10:3–7

I can know the truth by the power of the Holy Ghost.

The promise in Moroni 10:3–7 has changed the lives of millions of people around the world. How has it changed yours? Whether you are seeking to gain or to strengthen your testimony of the Book of Mormon, Moroni's invitation applies to you. As you read Moroni 10:3–7, consider reading more carefully than you have in the past. You could examine each phrase, asking yourself questions like these: What does this mean? How can I do this better? What experiences have I had with this? How has the Holy Ghost manifested the truth of the Book of Mormon to me?

Also think about someone who needs to hear your testimony of the Book of Mormon. How will you help that person seek his or her own witness?

MORONI 10:8–25

"Deny not the gifts of God."

There are many ways a person might "deny . . . the gifts of God" (Moroni 10:8). Some people deny that these gifts even exist. Others might deny that they have spiritual gifts but recognize them in other people. Still others deny their gifts by simply neglecting them or failing to develop them.

As you read Moroni 10:8–25, look for truths that will help you discover your spiritual gifts and use them with greater power to bless yourself and others. Seek insights about the gifts God has given you or the gifts He wants you to seek. Why is it important to "remember that every good gift cometh of Christ"? (Moroni 10:18).

Consider also this counsel from Elder John C. Pingree Jr.: "So how do we come to know our gifts? We can reference our patriarchal blessing, ask those who know us best, and personally identify what we are naturally good at and enjoy. Most important, we can ask God (see James 1:5; D&C 112:10). He knows our gifts, since He gave them to us" ("I Have a Work for Thee," *Ensign* or *Liahona,* Nov. 2017, 33).

See Guide to the Scriptures, "Gifts of the Spirit," scriptures.ChurchofJesusChrist.org.

MORONI 10:30–33

I can be perfected through the grace of Jesus Christ.

Moroni's admonition to "come unto Christ" involves more than learning about Him or thinking about Him more often or even trying harder to keep His commandments, as important as these things are. Rather, this is an invitation to come unto Christ in the most complete sense possible—to become as He is. As you read Moroni 10:30–33, notice phrases that help you understand what it means to come to Christ completely, such as "lay hold upon *every* good gift," "deny yourselves of *all* ungodliness," and, of course, "be *perfected* in him" (italics added).

How is this possible? Look for answers in Moroni 10:30–33. What is the Spirit telling you that you should do to more completely "come unto Christ, and be perfected in him"?

See Omni 1:26; Guide to the Scriptures, "Perfect," scriptures.ChurchofJesusChrist.org.

Ideas for Family Scripture Study and Family Home Evening

As you read the scriptures with your family, the Spirit can help you know what principles to emphasize and discuss in order to meet the needs of your family. Here are some ideas.

Moroni 10. Read this chapter together, looking for every time Moroni used the word *exhort*. List or mark what Moroni is exhorting—or strongly encouraging—us to do. What can we do to follow his exhortations?

Moroni 10:3. What have we learned about the Lord's mercy as we read the Book of Mormon this year? How has the Lord been merciful to our family?

Moroni 10:3–5. After reading these verses, you might ask family members to share how they have come to know that the Book of Mormon is true. Consider singing together a song about seeking for truth, such as "Search, Ponder, and Pray"

(*Children's Songbook,* 109). You might also invite family members to record their testimonies in a family journal.

Moroni 10:8–18. Christmas is a natural time to think about receiving gifts. Perhaps family members could wrap gifts for each other that represent the "gifts of God" mentioned in Moroni 10:9–16. These gifts could also represent other good gifts that come from Christ that they see in one another.

Moroni 10:27–29, 34. Family members could share what they would like to say to Moroni when they "meet [him] before the pleasing bar of the great Jehovah."

For more ideas for teaching children, see this week's outline in *Come, Follow Me—For Primary*.

Improving Personal Study

Look for Jesus Christ. The purpose of the Book of Mormon—and all scripture—is to testify of Jesus Christ. What do you learn about Jesus Christ in Moroni 10? What do you feel inspired to do to come unto Him?

Moroni Burying the Plates, by Jon McNaughton

Behold the Lamb of God, by Walter Rane

DECEMBER 21–27

Christmas

"HE SHALL COME INTO THE WORLD TO REDEEM HIS PEOPLE"

The Christmas season is a time to reflect on and express gratitude for the birth of our Savior, Jesus Christ. As you read and ponder this week about His birth and life, consider how your study of the Book of Mormon this year has strengthened your testimony that He is the Savior of the world. Record impressions that come to you.

RECORD YOUR IMPRESSIONS _____

_____

_____

From Nephi to Moroni, every Book of Mormon prophet was committed to the sacred purpose summarized on the book's title page: "The convincing of [all people] that Jesus is the Christ." One prophet saw Him as a premortal spirit, and another saw His birth and ministry in a vision. One stood on a wall to proclaim the signs of His birth and His death, and another knelt before His resurrected body, touching the wounds in His hands, feet, and side. All of them knew this essential truth: "There is no other way nor means whereby man can be saved, only through the atoning blood of Jesus Christ, who . . . cometh to redeem the world" (Helaman 5:9).

So during this Christmas season, as believers around the world celebrate the goodness and love of God in sending His Son, ponder how the Book of Mormon has strengthened your faith in Christ. As you think about His birth, ponder why He came and how His coming has changed your life. Then you can experience the true joy of Christmas—the gift that Jesus Christ gives to you.

Ideas for Personal Scripture Study

1 NEPHI 11:13–36; MOSIAH 3:5–10; HELAMAN 14:1–13; 3 NEPHI 1:4–22

Jesus Christ came to earth to be my Savior.

It's traditional to read the story of the Savior's birth in the New Testament at Christmastime, but you can also find moving prophecies of this sacred event in the Book of Mormon. For example, prophecies of the Savior's birth and ministry are found in 1 Nephi 11:13–36; Mosiah 3:5–10; Helaman 14:1–13; and 3 Nephi 1:4–22. What impressions about Jesus Christ come to you as you read these passages and contemplate the possible meanings of the signs of His birth? How do the testimonies of these prophets in ancient America strengthen your testimony of Christ and His mission?

See also Matthew 1:18–25; 2; Luke 2.

2 NEPHI 2:6; ALMA 7:7–13; 11:40; HELAMAN 5:9; 14:16–17

Jesus Christ is the Redeemer of all mankind.

We would have no reason to celebrate the birth of Jesus Christ were it not for His atoning sacrifice, through which He saves us from sin and death, comforts us in afflictions, and helps us "be perfected in Him" (Moroni 10:32). What have you learned from the Book of Mormon this year about the Savior's power to redeem you? Do any stories or teachings stand out to you? Consider what the following examples teach you about the Savior's redeeming mission: 2 Nephi 2:6; Alma 7:7–13; 11:40; and Helaman 5:9; 14:16–17. What do you feel inspired to do to show Him your gratitude? (Christmas.ComeuntoChrist.org has some ideas that can get you started.)

1 NEPHI 6:4; 19:18; 2 NEPHI 25:23, 26; 33:4, 10

The Book of Mormon testifies of Jesus Christ.

"Another Testament of Jesus Christ" is more than just a subtitle for the Book of Mormon; it is a statement of its divine purpose. Ponder what you learn from the following scriptures about the Book of Mormon's mission to testify of Christ: 1 Nephi 6:4; 19:18; and 2 Nephi 25:23, 26; 33:4, 10.

Consider recording in a journal how studying the Book of Mormon this year has brought you closer to Christ. The following prompts might help:

- "Something new I learned about the Savior this year was . . ."
- "Reading [verses about the Savior] changed the way I . . ."
- "My favorite person [or story] in the Book of Mormon taught me that the Savior . . ."

Ideas for Family Scripture Study and Family Home Evening

As you read the scriptures with your family, the Spirit can help you know what principles to emphasize and discuss in order to meet the needs of your family. Here are some ideas.

1 Nephi 11:13–23; Mosiah 3:5–10; Helaman 14:1–13; 3 Nephi 1:4–22. Children might enjoy drawing pictures of what they hear as you read the stories of Christ's birth and ministry in 1 Nephi 11:13–23; Mosiah 3:5–10; Helaman 14:1–13; and 3 Nephi 1:4–22. Then your children could retell the stories using the pictures they have drawn.

"He Is the Gift." To help your family focus on the gift Heavenly Father gave us by sending His

Son, you could wrap a picture of Jesus Christ like a Christmas present. Family members could talk about favorite Christmas gifts they have received or hope to receive. Then they could unwrap the picture of Christ and discuss how He has been a precious gift for us. The video "He Is the Gift" (ChurchofJesusChrist.org) could help you discuss how you can discover, embrace, and share the gift of the Savior as a family this Christmas.

Your family might also benefit from thinking about a "gift" they would like to give the Savior, such as making an effort to be kinder to others or working to overcome a bad habit. Consider inviting family members to write down their ideas, wrap them like a gift, and place their gifts around a picture of the Savior.

The Christmas Spirit. It might be fun to plan activities your family can do in the days leading up to Christmas to feel the Spirit of Christ, such as serving someone or singing Christmas hymns together. (For ideas, see Christmas.ComeuntoChrist.org.)

For more ideas for teaching children, see this week's outline in *Come, Follow Me—For Primary.*

Improving Our Teaching

Follow up on invitations to act. "When you follow up on an invitation to act, you show [your family members] that you care about them and how the gospel is blessing their lives. You also give them opportunities to share their experiences, which strengthens their commitment and allows them to support one another in living the gospel" (*Teaching in the Savior's Way*, 35).

Nephi's Vision of the Virgin Mary, by Judith A. Mehr

How Does the Spirit Witness to Me That the Book of Mormon Is True?

You may have heard about Moroni's promise to all who read the Book of Mormon: "If ye shall ask with a sincere heart, with real intent, having faith in Christ, he will manifest the truth of [the Book of Mormon] unto you, by the power of the Holy Ghost" (Moroni 10:4). But what does it mean to know the truth "by the power of the Holy Ghost"? How can you know when the Holy Ghost is speaking to you?

It may be helpful to remember that the Holy Ghost communicates with us in ways that are very different from the ways we are used to communicating with each other. But your Heavenly Father wants to help you learn to recognize the Spirit. He has given you the Book of Mormon, where several faithful servants describe their experiences with the voice of the Lord.

For example, Nephi told his brothers that the Lord had spoken to them "in a still small voice," though not necessarily a voice they could hear with their ears. In fact, Nephi said his brothers were "past feeling" and could not *feel* his words" (1 Nephi 17:45, italics added). Enos described the answer to his prayers as "the voice of the Lord" coming "into [his] mind" (Enos 1:10). And consider these words describing the voice that came from heaven when the resurrected Savior appeared in the land Bountiful: "It was not a harsh voice, neither was it a loud voice; nevertheless, . . . it did pierce them to the very soul, and did cause their hearts to burn" (3 Nephi 11:3).

Perhaps you've had experiences similar to these, or maybe your experiences have been different. The Holy Ghost communicates in a variety of ways, and revelation can come to each of us differently. And when the Spirit is in our lives, we will see His influence upon us in many ways. The Apostle Paul spoke of "the fruit of the Spirit"—feelings of "love, joy, peace, longsuffering, gentleness, goodness, faith, meekness, temperance," among many others (Galatians 5:22–23).

Here are some other teachings and examples from the Book of Mormon about the Holy Ghost. As you read them, you may see that the Holy Ghost has been speaking to you more than you realize, bearing witness to you that the Book of Mormon truly is the word of God.

Gratitude and Joy

The Book of Mormon opens with the prophet Lehi seeing a marvelous vision. In this vision, he was given a book and invited to read. "As he read," the record says, "he was filled with the Spirit of the Lord." This experience led Lehi to praise God for His "power, and goodness, and mercy," and Lehi's "soul did rejoice, and his whole heart was filled" (1 Nephi 1:12, 14–15).

Have you ever had a similar experience? Has reading the Book of Mormon ever filled your heart with gratitude for God's goodness and mercy? Have passages in the Book of Mormon ever caused your soul to rejoice? These feelings are the influence of the Spirit, testifying to you that the words you are reading come from God and teach His truth.

A Changed Heart

After preaching a remarkable sermon about the Atonement of Jesus Christ (see Mosiah 2–4), King Benjamin wanted to know if his people "believed the words which he had spoken unto them." They responded that they did believe his message. Why? "Because of the Spirit of the Lord Omnipotent, which has wrought a mighty change in us, or in our hearts, that we have no more disposition to do evil, but to do good continually" (Mosiah 5:1–2).

Maybe you have noticed something similar in your heart as you have read the Book of Mormon. For instance, you may have felt inspired to be a better person, to turn away from sin, or to do something kind for someone. This is the spiritual witness you are looking for that the book is inspired of God. For as Mormon taught, "Every thing which inviteth and enticeth to do good, and to love God, and to serve him, is inspired of God" (Moroni 7:13; see also 2 Nephi 33:4, 10; Alma 19:33; Ether 4:11–12).

An Enlightened Mind

When Alma wanted to help the Zoramites "experiment upon [his] words" and know for themselves whether his testimony was true, he compared the word of God to a seed: "If ye give place, that a seed may be planted in your heart," he explained, "it will begin to swell within your breasts; and when you feel these swelling motions, ye will begin to say within yourselves—It must needs be that this is a good seed, or that the word is good, for it beginneth to enlarge my soul; yea, it beginneth to enlighten my understanding, yea, it beginneth to be delicious to me" (Alma 32:27–28).

You "give place" in your heart for the words of the Book of Mormon when you allow them to influence your life and guide your choices. And how will these words "enlarge [your] soul" and "enlighten [your] understanding"? You might sense that you are becoming spiritually stronger. You might feel more loving and open toward others. You might also notice that you understand things better, especially spiritual things—almost as if a light is shining in your mind. And you might agree that the doctrine taught in the Book of Mormon is "delicious." Such feelings can help you understand that you have truly received a spiritual witness of truth, as Alma declared: "O then, is not this real? I say unto you, Yea, because it is light; and whatsoever is light, is good, because it is discernible, therefore ye must know that it is good" (Alma 32:35).

You Do Not Have to Wonder

These are just some of the ways in which the Spirit communicates. There are many others. Keep looking for opportunities to listen to the voice of the Spirit, and you will receive His ongoing, confirming witness of the truthfulness of the Book of Mormon.

President Russell M. Nelson has promised: "You don't have to wonder about what is true. You do not have to wonder whom you can safely trust. Through personal revelation, you can receive your own witness that the Book of Mormon is the word of God, that Joseph Smith is a prophet, and that this is the Lord's Church. Regardless of what others may say or do, no one can ever take away a witness borne to your heart and mind about what is true" ("Revelation for the Church, Revelation for Our Lives," *Ensign* or *Liahona,* May 2018, 95).

"Plain and Precious Truths"

The Book of Mormon was prepared to come forth during the last days, a time of widespread confusion about doctrine, or God's eternal truth. Part of that book's divine purpose is, as Nephi foresaw, to "establish the truth of the [Bible]," to "make known the plain and precious things" that have been lost over the centuries, and to "make known to all kindreds, tongues, and people, that the Lamb of God is the Son of the Eternal Father, and the Savior of the world" (1 Nephi 13:40).

The Book of Mormon reveals eternal truths that were lost during the Apostasy and adds a second, clarifying witness to many truths taught in the Bible. Here are just a few of those truths. Look for these and other plain and precious truths as you study the Book of Mormon.

The Godhead

- Heavenly Father, Jesus Christ, and the Holy Ghost are separate beings but one in purpose (see 3 Nephi 11:32, 36).

- The resurrected Savior has a tangible body (see 3 Nephi 11:10–17).

Additional scriptures about the Godhead:
2 Nephi 31:6–8; Ether 12:41

The Atonement of Jesus Christ

- Jesus Christ suffered for our sins and afflictions so He would know how to succor us (see Alma 7:11–13).

- We can become perfected through the grace of Jesus Christ (see Moroni 10:32–33).

Additional scriptures about the Savior's Atonement:
1 Nephi 10:6; 2 Nephi 2:6–9; Jacob 4:11–12; Mosiah 3:1–19; Alma 34:8–16

The Plan of Salvation

- The Fall of Adam and Eve was an essential part of Heavenly Father's plan (see 2 Nephi 2:22–27).

- Opposition was necessary for us to be able to exercise agency (see 2 Nephi 2:11–16).

- We will be judged according to our works and the desires of our hearts (see Alma 41:3–7).

- The "lake of fire and brimstone" is symbolic of the anguish of the unrepentant (see 2 Nephi 9:16–19; Mosiah 3:24–27).

Additional scriptures about the plan of salvation:
2 Nephi 9:11–26; Alma 22:12–14; 34:31–35; 42:1–26

The Apostasy and the Restoration

- The Great Apostasy occurred because of wickedness and unbelief (see Mormon 8:28, 31–41).

- The Book of Mormon establishes the truths taught in the Bible (see 1 Nephi 13:19–41; 2 Nephi 3:12).

- Christ's Church should be called in His name (see 3 Nephi 27:3–9).

Additional scriptures about the Apostasy:
1 Nephi 13:1–9, 24–29; 2 Nephi 27–28

Additional scriptures about the Restoration:
1 Nephi 14:7–12; 22:7–11; 2 Nephi 3:7–24; 25:17–18

Prophets and Revelation

- All prophets testify of Jesus Christ
  (see Mosiah 13:33–35).

- A knowledge of spiritual truth comes through the
  Holy Ghost (see Alma 5:45–47).

- The Bible does not contain all of God's word (see
  2 Nephi 29:10–13).

- Revelation from God has not ceased in our day
  (see Mormon 9:7–9).

Additional scriptures about prophets: 1 Nephi 22:1–2;
Mosiah 8:16–18; Helaman 13:24–33

Additional scriptures about revelation: Jacob 4:8; Alma
12:9–11; 17:2–3; Moroni 10:5

Priesthood

- Priesthood holders were called and prepared
  from the foundation of the world
  (see Alma 13:1–3).

- A person must receive authority from God to
  preach the gospel (see Mosiah 23:17).

Additional scriptures about the priesthood: Mosiah
18:17–20; Alma 13; Helaman 10:7

Ordinances and Covenants

- Baptism is essential to receive eternal life
  (see 2 Nephi 31:4–13, 17–18).

- Baptism must be performed by immersion
  (see 3 Nephi 11:23–27).

- Little children have no need to be baptized
  (see Moroni 8:8–12).

- Ordinances must be administered according to
  the commandments of Christ by someone with
  proper authority (see Mosiah 18:17–18;
  3 Nephi 11:21–27; Moroni 4:1).

Additional scriptures about ordinances: Mosiah 18:8–
17; 21:33–35; Alma 13:16; 3 Nephi 18:1–11;
Moroni 2–6; 8:4–26

Additional scriptures about covenants: 2 Nephi 11:5;
Mosiah 5:1–9; Alma 24:17–18

Marriage and Family

- Husbands and wives should love one another
  (see Jacob 3:5–7).

- Parents should raise up their children unto the
  Lord (see 1 Nephi 7:1).

Additional scriptures about marriage and family:
1 Nephi 1:1; 2 Nephi 25:26; Jacob 2:23–28; Enos 1:1;
Mosiah 4:14–15; 3 Nephi 18:21

Commandments

- The Lord will prepare a way for us to accomplish
  His commandments (see 1 Nephi 3:7).

- God promises to bless us if we keep His commandments (see Mosiah 2:22–24).

Additional scriptures about commandments:
1 Nephi 17:3; 22:30–31; Alma 37:13, 35; 50:20

The Three Witnesses

For more than five years—from the time of the angel Moroni's first visit to Joseph Smith until 1829—Joseph was the only person who was allowed to see the gold plates. This led to intense criticism and persecution from those who believed he was deceiving people. So imagine the joy Joseph felt when, as he translated the Book of Mormon, he learned that the Lord would allow others to see the plates and that they too would "testify to the truth of the book and the things therein" (2 Nephi 27:12–14; see also 2 Nephi 11:3; Ether 5:2–4).

In June 1829, Oliver Cowdery, David Whitmer, and Martin Harris asked for permission to be the three witnesses of whom the Book of Mormon prophesied. The Lord granted them their desire (see D&C 17) and sent an angel, who showed them the plates. These men became known as the Three Witnesses, and their written testimony is included in every copy of the Book of Mormon.[1]

President Dallin H. Oaks explained why the testimony of the Three Witnesses is so compelling: "The testimony of the Three Witnesses to the Book of Mormon stands forth in great strength. Each of the three had ample reason and opportunity to renounce his testimony if it had been false, or to equivocate on details if any had been inaccurate. As is well known, because of disagreements or jealousies involving other leaders of the Church, each one of these three witnesses was excommunicated from The Church of Jesus Christ of Latter-day Saints by about eight years after the publication of their testimony. All three went their separate ways, with no common interest to support a collusive effort. Yet to the end of their lives—periods ranging from 12 to 50 years after their excommunications—not one of these witnesses deviated from his published testimony or said anything that cast any shadow on its truthfulness."[2]

Until the end of their lives, the Three Witnesses were unwavering in their faithfulness to their testimony of the Book of Mormon.

Oliver Cowdery

After being rebaptized into the Church and shortly before his death, Oliver visited with a missionary, Elder Jacob Gates, who was passing through Richmond, Missouri, on his way to serve a mission in England. Elder Gates asked Oliver about his testimony of the Book of Mormon. Elder Gates's son recounted Oliver's reaction:

"To question him thus seemed to touch Oliver very deeply. He answered not a word, but arose from his easy chair, went to the book case, took down a Book of Mormon of the first edition, turned to the testimony of the Three Witnesses, and read in the most solemn manner the words to which he had subscribed his name, nearly twenty years before. Facing my father, he said: 'Jacob, I want you to remember what I say to you. I am a dying man, and what would it profit me to tell you a lie? I know,' said he, 'that this Book of Mormon was translated by the gift and power of God. My eyes saw, my ears heard, and my understanding was touched, and I know that whereof I testified is true. It was no dream, no vain imagination of the mind—it was real.'"[3]

David Whitmer

In his later years, David Whitmer became aware of rumors that he had denied his testimony of the Book of Mormon. In response to these accusations, David reaffirmed his testimony in a letter that was published in the local newspaper, the *Richmond Conservator:*

"That the world may know the truth, I wish now, standing, as it were, in the very sunset of life, and in the fear of God once for all, to make this public statement:

"That I have never at any time denied that testimony, or any part thereof, which has so long since been published with that Book, as one of the three witnesses. Those who know me best, well know that I have always adhered to that testimony. And that no man may be misled or doubt my present views in regard to the same, I do again affirm the truth of all of my statements, as then made and published.

"'He that hath an ear to hear, let him hear,' it was no delusion! What is written is written—and he that readeth let him understand."[4]

Martin Harris

Like Oliver Cowdery, Martin Harris left the Church for a time but was eventually rebaptized. In his later years, he was known to carry a copy of the Book of Mormon under his arm and testify of its truthfulness to all who would listen: "I know the Book of Mormon to be verily true. And although all men should deny the truth of that book, I dare not do it. My heart is fixed. O God, my heart is fixed! I could not know more truly or certainly than I do."[5]

George Godfrey, an acquaintance of Martin's, wrote: "A few hours before his death . . . I asked [Martin] if he did not feel that there was an element at least, of fraudulence and deception in the things that were written and told of the coming forth of the Book of Mormon, and he replied as he had always done . . . and said: 'The Book of Mormon is no fake. I know what I know. I have seen what I have seen and I have heard what I have heard. I have seen the gold plates from which the Book of Mormon is written. An angel appeared to me and others and testified to the truthfulness of the record, and had I been willing to have perjured myself and sworn falsely to the testimony I now bear I could have been a rich man, but I could not have testified other than I have done and am now doing for these things are true.'"[6]

"As Many Witnesses as Seemeth Him Good"

The testimonies of the Three Witnesses are especially impressive considering their experiences both in and out of the Church.[7] Through it all, Oliver, David, and Martin never stopped testifying of what they had experienced and bearing witness that the Book of Mormon was translated by the gift and power of God. And they were not the only ones.

Anciently, Nephi declared, "The Lord God will proceed to bring forth the words of the book; and in the mouth of as many witnesses as seemeth him good will he establish his word" (2 Nephi 27:14). In addition to the Prophet Joseph Smith and the Three Witnesses, the Lord also chose eight other witnesses to view the plates. Their testimony is also included in every copy of the Book of Mormon. Like Oliver, David, and Martin, the Eight Witnesses remained true to their testimonies of the Book of Mormon and their witness of the gold plates.

William E. McLellin was an early convert to the Church who knew many of the witnesses of the Book of Mormon personally. William eventually left the Church, but he continued to be deeply affected by the compelling testimonies he had heard from the witnesses.

"Now I would ask," McLellin wrote toward the end of his life, "what will I do with such a cloud of faithful witnesses, bearing such a rational and yet solemn testimony? These men while in the prime of life, saw the vision of the angel, and bore their testimony to all people. And eight men saw the plates, and handled them. Hence these men all knew the things they declared to be positively true. And that too while they were young, and now when old they declare the same things."[8]

Even though we have not seen the gold plates as the Three Witnesses did, we can draw strength from their testimonies. Even when their reputations were challenged and their safety and lives were threatened because of their testimonies, these men of integrity courageously stayed true to their witness to the very end.

1. Read about their experience in *Saints: The Story of the Church of Jesus Christ in the Latter Days,* vol. 1, *The Standard of Truth, 1815–1846* (2018), 73–75.

2. Dallin H. Oaks, "The Witness: Martin Harris," *Ensign,* May 1999, 36.

3. Jacob F. Gates, "Testimony of Jacob Gates," *Improvement Era,* Mar. 1912, 418–19.

4. In Lyndon W. Cook, ed., *David Whitmer Interviews: A Restoration Witness* (1991), 79.

5. In Mitchell K. Schaefer, "The Testimony of Men: William E. McLellin and the Book of Mormon Witnesses," *BYU Studies,* vol. 50, no. 1 (2011), 108; capitalization standardized.

6. George Godfrey, "Testimony of Martin Harris" (unpublished manuscript), quoted in Eldin Ricks, *The Case of the Book of Mormon Witnesses* (1961), 65–66.

7. For example, see *Saints,* 1:182–83.

8. In Schaefer, "Testimony of Men," 110.

Suggested Music for Families

Families may choose to use the following hymns and children's songs during family scripture study or family home evening to support the doctrine taught in the Book of Mormon. Children will be singing many of these songs in their Primary classes and singing time.

January

December 30–January 5 (Introductory Pages of the Book of Mormon): "Book of Mormon Stories" (*Children's Songbook,* 118–19)

January 6–12 (1 Nephi 1–7): "Keep the Commandments" (*Children's Songbook,* 146–47)

January 13–19 (1 Nephi 8–10): "Search, Ponder, and Pray" (*Children's Songbook,* 109)

January 20–26 (1 Nephi 11–15): "The Iron Rod" (*Hymns,* no. 274)

February

January 27–February 2 (1 Nephi 16–22): "Nephi's Courage" (*Children's Songbook,* 120–21)

February 3–9 (2 Nephi 1–5): "Praise to the Man" (*Hymns,* no. 27)

February 10–16 (2 Nephi 6–10): "I Feel My Savior's Love" (*Children's Songbook,* 74–75)

February 17–23 (2 Nephi 11–25): "I Love to See the Temple" (*Children's Songbook,* 95)

March

February 24–March 1 (2 Nephi 26–30): "The Holy Ghost" (*Children's Songbook,* 105)

March 2–8 (2 Nephi 31–33): "When I Am Baptized" (*Children's Songbook,* 103)

March 9–15 (Jacob 1–4): "The Wise Man and the Foolish Man" (*Children's Songbook,* 281)

March 16–22 (Jacob 5–7): "Dare to Do Right" (*Children's Songbook,* 158)

March 23–March 29 (Enos–Words of Mormon): "A Child's Prayer" (*Children's Songbook,* 12–13)

April

March 30–April 12 (Easter): "Easter Hosanna" (*Children's Songbook,* 68–69)

April 13–19 (Mosiah 1–3): "When We're Helping" (*Children's Songbook,* 198)

April 20–26 (Mosiah 4–6): "Love One Another" (*Children's Songbook,* 136–37)

May

April 27–May 3 (Mosiah 7–10): "Book of Mormon Stories" (*Children's Songbook,* 118–19)

May 4–10 (Mosiah 11–17): "I Will Be Valiant" (*Children's Songbook,* 162)

May 11–17 (Mosiah 18–24): "Baptism" (*Children's Songbook,* 100–101)

May 18–24 (Mosiah 25–28): "Help Me, Dear Father" (*Children's Songbook,* 99)

May 25–31 (Mosiah 29–Alma 4): "Testimony" (*Hymns,* no. 137)

June

June 1–7 (Alma 5–7): "Come, Follow Me" (*Hymns,* no. 116)

June 8–14 (Alma 8–12): "We'll Bring the World His Truth" (*Children's Songbook,* 172–73)

June 15–21 (Alma 13–16): "Follow the Prophet" (*Children's Songbook,* 110–11)

June 22–28 (Alma 17–22): "I Want to Be a Missionary Now" (*Children's Songbook,* 168)

July

June 29–July 5 (Alma 23–29): "For Health and Strength" (*Children's Songbook,* 21)

July 6–12 (Alma 30–31): "My Heavenly Father Loves Me" (*Children's Songbook,* 228–29)

July 13–19 (Alma 32–35): "Faith" (*Children's Songbook,* 96–97)

July 20–26 (Alma 36–38): "As I Search the Holy Scriptures" (*Hymns,* no. 277)

August

July 27–August 2 (Alma 39–42): "Repentance" (*Children's Songbook,* 98)

August 3–9 (Alma 43–52): "Home Can Be a Heaven on Earth" (*Hymns,* no. 298)

August 10–16 (Alma 53–63): "We'll Bring the World His Truth" (*Children's Songbook,* 172–73)

August 17–23 (Helaman 1–6): "The Still Small Voice" (*Children's Songbook,* 106–7)

August 24–30 (Helaman 7–12): "Follow the Prophet" (*Children's Songbook,* 110–11)

September

August 31–September 6 (Helaman 13–16): "Samuel Tells of the Baby Jesus" (*Children's Songbook,* 36)

September 7–13 (3 Nephi 1–7): "I'm Trying to Be like Jesus" (*Children's Songbook,* 78–79)

September 14–20 (3 Nephi 8–11): "This Is My Beloved Son" (*Children's Songbook,* 76)

September 21–27 (3 Nephi 12–16): "The Wise Man and the Foolish Man" (*Children's Songbook,* 281)

October

September 28–October 11 (3 Nephi 17–19): "Reverently, Quietly" (*Children's Songbook,* 26)

October 12–18 (3 Nephi 20–26): "Families Can Be Together Forever" (*Children's Songbook,* 188)

October 19–25 (3 Nephi 27–4 Nephi): "The Church of Jesus Christ" (*Children's Songbook,* 77)

November

October 26–November 1 (Mormon 1–6): "Jesus Said Love Everyone" (*Children's Songbook,* 61)

November 2–8 (Mormon 7–9): "Stand for the Right" (*Children's Songbook,* 159)

November 9–15 (Ether 1–5): "Head, Shoulders, Knees, and Toes" (*Children's Songbook,* 275)

November 16–22 (Ether 6–11): "I Thank Thee, Dear Father" (*Children's Songbook,* 7)

November 23–29 (Ether 12–15): "Faith" (*Children's Songbook,* 96–97)

December

November 30–December 6 (Moroni 1–6): "Help Me, Dear Father" (*Children's Songbook,* 99)

December 7–13 (Moroni 7–9): "I Will Follow God's Plan" (*Children's Songbook,* 164–65)

December 14–20 (Moroni 10): "Search, Ponder, and Pray" (*Children's Songbook,* 109)

December 21–27 (Christmas): "Away in a Manger" (*Children's Songbook,* 42–43)